CREATE EMPATHY

*How to influence people and create relationships
with effective persuasive communication
and the art of listening*

- Liam Dave Patterson -

© Copyright 2020 - All rights reserved

The content contained within this book may not be reproduced, duplicated or transmitted without direct written permission from the author or the publisher.

Under no circumstances will any blame or legal responsibility be held against the publisher, or author, for any damages, reparation, or monetary loss due to the information contained within this book. Either directly or indirectly.

Legal Notice:

This book is copyright protected. This book is only for personal use. You cannot amend, distribute, sell, use, quote or paraphrase any part, or the content within this book, without the consent of the author or publisher.

Disclaimer Notice:

Please note the information contained within this document is for educational and entertainment purposes only. All effort has been executed to present accurate, up to date, and reliable, complete information. No warranties of any kind are declared or implied. Readers acknowledge that the author is not engaging in the rendering of legal, financial, medical or professional advice. The content within this book has been derived from various sources. Please consult a licensed professional before attempting any techniques outlined in this book.

By reading this document, the reader agrees that under no circumstances is the author responsible for any losses, direct or indirect, which are incurred as a result of the use of information contained within this document, including, but not limited to errors, omissions or inaccuracies.

TABLE OF CONTENTS

Introduction
Chapter 1: We're in the "Fast Communication Era"
Chapter 2: Simple Communication - When Less is More
Chapter 3: Art of Listening
Chapter 4: How to Manage People's Attention
Chapter 5: Being Seen, Heard and Understood
Chapter 6: Create Empathy - Charismatic Communication
Chapter 7: The Power Words to Use in Communication
Chapter 8: Win People to Your Way - The Power of Persuasion
Chapter 9: Boost Enthusiasm Among Your Colleagues
Chapter 10: Anticipate Objections and Manage Relationship Rules
Chapter 11: Make Friends Quickly and Easily
Chapter 12: What Men and Women Want
Chapter 13: The Art of Storytelling - How to Tell Stories That Sell
Chapter 14: Laws of Persuasion and Attraction
Chapter 15: Create Your Story Brand
Chapter 16: Communication in Public Speaking
Chapter 17: Communication in One to One Business Sales
Chapter 18: Communication in Meetings
Chapter 19: Communication on Social Media
Chapter 20: Communication on Social Video
Chapter 21: Communication on Websites
Chapter 22: Communication on Instant Messaging
Chapter 23: How to Organize a Winning Business Speech

INTRODUCTION

We all want to be thought of as likable because that means you'll get ahead both in your social life and in business settings. You see that person who is always the "life of the party," and you compare yourself to them. You might think, "is it their way with words, charisma, or other secrets to life that they have already figured out?" It's actually a much simpler concept than that. It all lies in how well you can tap into your empathy.

Empathy has long been thought of as the ability to understand what others are feeling- "put yourself in someone else's shoes." While this is partially true, there is much more to empathy than that. It is something that can benefit you greatly in your pursuit of success in all areas of your life. When you have mastered empathy, not only do you know how someone would feel about something that has already happened to them, but you will be able to predict how others might react to what you are thinking about saying or doing. When you think about it that way, empathy gives you the power to look into the future!

You'll be able to tell which behaviors will make your first impression go over well and which ones are off-putting and therefore need to be avoided. All of these bits of knowledge will add up to you knowing how to behave and what to say in any social situation. In turn, means you will conquer all of them.

WHY THIS BOOK

Empathy is so important to social interactions that it is considered one of the five pieces of emotional intelligence, which are the unofficial guidelines for how to talk to others successfully. This is not meant to scare you. The fact that you are reading this book shows that you already have the building blocks for empathy. When someone tells you, they're going through a difficult time, and it hurts your feelings to hear that, it means the capacity for empathy is within you.

Being liked by others has gone beyond just being a luxury in the modern world. It is necessary if you are going to make it in your career. The connections you have and what potential employers think of your personality plays an integral role in being promoted and considered for leadership positions. There are a number of world leaders who did not make remarkable grades in school, but instead got ahead based on the fact that others feel like they can relate to them "the guy you could have a drink with."

When you utilize, you tend to the emotional needs of others, which makes them more inclined to do the same for you. It creates a symbiotic relationship. However, there is a caveat to this. What makes this art so complicated is that you also do not want to give off the impression that you are nice to someone just to get something out of them, because that is off-putting for anyone.

This might sound confusing, but you don't need to worry. As you go through this book, you will learn all of the things that come into play when you are trying to perfect your empathy skills, including:

- Communicating with others
- What listening really is, not just hearing the words

- How to effectively speak to people of different demographics
- How to give an oral presentation that keeps people interested
- Cutting out unnecessary information when you speak
- How to read nonverbal cues from others
- Building a connection with other people
- How to put your best foot forward in a different social situation
- How to upkeep your mental health so you can be successful
- Communication when face-to-face isn't possible
- How to be persuasive without being manipulative
- How to know what is appropriate to say before you say it
- Responding to criticism
- How to make up for it when you have made a mistake
- And much more!

You do not need to feel overwhelmed by all of this. You are already on the right track because the desire to learn and master empathy is within you. Today is the start of a change in your life, and I am going to help you go through it. In fact, I think as you read this book, you will be surprised at how much you already know. You are already an empathetic person. Now you are going to work at being a master at the subject. Give this book a read to begin your path to success!

CHAPTER 1

WE'RE IN THE "FAST COMMUNICATION ERA"

We live in an age where we do so much of our communication electronically. Everything from communicating with service providers, filing a claim on our insurance, applying for a job, talking to our colleagues, family, and friends to meeting someone to date can all be done online. We chat with people in video games who we will never meet, and our only connection is a contest online through our avatars.

It is no secret that there are more avenues of communication. However, another thing to think about is the impact this has on the way we talk to one another. In the most obvious sense, it has resulted in slang, acronyms, and other verbiage that would not exist without it, because we often try to fit our messages into the smallest sentences possible.

You may have heard an older person say how people do not talk anymore and that there is an absence of respect and dignity that we should give one another. They are told that they need to get on board with the new way of things and that they are old fashioned. When they do, they are laughed at because they do not know all of the abbreviations like LOL, OMG, ROFL, and IRL and because they tend to spell everything out.

However, etiquette should not be lost. The way you greet someone should be pleasant, instead of just launching into a barrage of what you want or a grievance. Propriety should be considered when speaking electronically with people, just the same as when speaking face to face, such as:

- Listen/read and thoroughly consider what the other person is saying or asking
- Let there be a pause
- Answer one question before launching into the next
- Do not interrupt, can be translated to let the other person speak
- Exercise tact
- A conversation is shared, and it is not a competition

Remember that you are speaking to another person, and it is not just "words on a screen." Use the same empathy that you expect. Just because you are typing with someone you may not know, there is no need to be rude. For example, your friend texts and invites you to meet for lunch at a restaurant. You do not like the restaurant, you would like to go somewhere different, or you feel that you will be driving the bulk of the distance. Your first impulse may be to fire off a text with an economy of words that does sound nice to your friend. Maybe they ask to meet another time, and you just answer affirmatively.

What you may be forgetting is that people read what you write and add voice inflection. You may not mean to hurt your friend's feelings, but if you forget to use proper feelings and manners, you can damage relationships.

While you are texting or chatting with someone, you cannot see their non-verbal social cues. You cannot see their facial expressions, whether they laugh at something you said, meaning to be funny, or if their face has suddenly fallen because they feel you have been too abrupt with them.

Do not let yourself off the hook by believing yourself to be in a hurry. If you do not have time to speak, or are already in a conversation with another person, let it be known that you need to talk at another time. Alternatively, if they cannot talk at the moment, let them know that it is okay and suggest another time.

That way, no one is trying to carry on two conversations at once. Empathy can certainly be lost if you try that.

It can get overwhelming trying to keep up with every communication method. There are so many social media forms, and then you have your text messages and emails to think about. This is why you need to take time at the end of the day to make sure you have gotten in touch with the people you have told would hear from you. This means a lot to people. Let's say you work in IT, and you recently had a customer come to you because they were having battery issues. After you fix it and you see that their phone is functional, do not let that be the end of your interaction with them. Wait a couple of days and then follow up with them. Ask them if their battery is still working well and if there is anything else you can help them with. This will lead you to get more positive reviews because customers will see you as being attentive and someone who goes above and beyond to help. An employee who checks in, lets their client know that they care and that their money was not spent in vain.

Finally, make sure to say the name of the person you are talking to from time to time, especially when you are talking through a messaging device. This might not seem like much, but it will subconsciously remind you of who you are talking to. Your previous interactions and their feelings will be at the forefront of your mind. This will encourage you to treat them like an individual person, which is a concept we must preserve in the fast communication era.

CHAPTER 2

SIMPLE COMMUNICATION: WHEN LESS IS MORE

We all want to be thought of as eloquent speakers, and this is an excellent technique to learn. However, you also need to learn the art of being short and concise with your language. There are times that it is powerful to speak for a long time and send a repetitive message. There are other times where using simpler language is the way to go.

There is a time and place for larger words, and in certain times they can show off intelligence, but there is a point where this gets tedious. People who use overly flowery language can give off the impression of being pompous or elitist like they are trying to talk over everyone's head. Have you ever had someone go off on a tangent about something you knew nothing about? They were using terms you haven't been taught about, and therefore you were unable to follow their train of thought. It probably also made you feel poorly about yourself because you couldn't understand.

This is why we need to make sure we do not do this to other people. Think about when you were in school, and you were assigned an essay to write. Your teacher probably told you something along the lines of "you need to write as if you are explaining this to a five-year-old." This was not to imply that the reader is not intelligent. It was to make you remember to keep your communication clear.

When you are introducing a new concept to someone, take it easy on the technical jargon. Say you are teaching someone to play the guitar. They are not going to know about chords, frets, and so on. Start by teaching them about the strings and what purpose each serves since everyone is familiar with the idea of strings on a guitar. Then you can start by teaching them some of the most commonly used chords like C, D, and F major. These should be mastered before going into highly complex chords. It can be discouraging for someone to overcomplicate things and jump ahead too much.

When you are telling someone information, give them a brief summary of it. When you try to give them a recap of every detail, your message will come across as muddled, and you will overwhelm them. If someone were asking you to tell them what a certain movie was about, you would not recite the entire film word for word. You would give them the highlights of it.

Keeping things simple also means decluttering your life. A couple of times per year, it is a good idea to declutter your house. Things pile up, including papers, magazines, clothes, etc. and we need to reduce the amount of "stuff" we keep. If you have not worn something within six months, or if it no longer fits, donate it to charity. Food items should be examined, and if it is past its expiration date, pitch it. Take note of things you may be buying, but you do not tend to eat. Those items are in your way and cluttering your cabinet space so that you cannot see what you have that you actually will eat.

Clear off your working spaces and surfaces of bed-side tables. Do not let it get to the point that you have no free space to set down your water glass.

Do you find yourself with too little time because you have taken on things that you honestly do not have time for? Maybe you fear by saying no, you are letting people down and/or you may be regarded unfavorably. You want to be known as a do-gooder. However, if you take on too much, you wind up stressed out and overworked. Learn to say no when you are at your limit.

There is a certain point at which perfectionism is not your friend. Being a perfectionist can keep you focused on a certain task, unable to move forward to others, thereby wasting your time. Certainly, everyone wants to do things well. However, be sure you can discern the fine line between repeating a task because it needs to happen and when the improvement is below your margin for error.

Your telephone can complicate your life to a large degree. While you want to remain accessible for people, it's important to schedule your most important task-oriented work at the start of the day so your mind will be fresh. You can check your emails after that. Constantly monitoring your email and responding right away can take your attention away from your work at hand. Remember that many times, people will resolve their own issues within a 30-minute timeframe if you do not answer them right away. It is honorable to be known as a go-to person, but if you focus your efforts too strongly towards your inbox, you are probably neglecting work that needs concentration.

Finally, simplify your life by cutting ties with habits and people that are unhealthy for you. If you find yourself being consistently nervous about your next conversation with a certain person, that is a good indicator that this connection is causing you more harm than good.

You need to know whether a situation calls for more or less speech.

When you are at a meeting at work, you want to be an active participant. You do not want to just sit there because it could give your employer the impression that you are just waiting for the meeting to be over so you can leave, which will not show dedication to the company. Volunteer to take notes or anything else that could make you of assistance. Answer questions. Offer solutions. They do not need to be perfect; it just shows that you are eager to make a contribution. If there is a call for volunteers to do something, offer to be among them.

Now, let's say your friend comes to you with a problem and needs to vent about it. This is a time when you need to curtail your speech. You might feel tempted to offer advice or state your opinion on something, but hold back. This will impede their ability to confide in you. I know you have good intentions in doing this, but when a person comes to you to vent, they want to let out things they have needed to say. They are not always looking for a solution. Sometimes they just want to sort things out in their mind in a safe and non-judgmental setting, which can sometimes lead to a solution because then they can see things with more clarity.

When you are giving a speech, it is easy to feel pressure to give the same amount of time to each point for the sake of being even. However, that is easier said than done, and it is not always possible. Sometimes there is only so much you can say about a subject. On the other hand, another one might need more time if it is to be fully addressed. Importantly, slow down your speech and avoid rushing through the points. That is more important than even spacing.

Think about who you are giving a speech to. Certain age groups will be willing to listen to a lengthy speech more so than others. Get a feel for the personality of your audience. Do they want to hear jokes and entertaining stories, or are they just here to get the facts?

There is something to the saying, "less is more." This means that sometimes you can convey just as strong of a message with fewer words. Let's say you are a teacher, and you want to introduce a new concept to your students. You might think using a set of multiple examples will get it through to them more thoroughly, but this will be more cumbersome to try to explain it. If you use one example, you will be able to flesh it out more. You will not need to juggle so many things. Also, it allows time for the students to try a problem on their own. Often people learn best when they do something, learning from their mistakes.

Say you are giving a presentation about the life of a historical figure. If you were to try to incorporate everything that ever happened in their life into your speech, this would come across as rambling, and your speech would be discombobulated. Come up with several defining moments of their life. What are they the most known for? Discuss the work they did during their life and how it affects the world today.

Perhaps you know an interesting fact about their personal life that most people do not know. That can pique the audience's interest and keep their attention fully on what you have to say.

When you have said everything you need to say, do not feel pressure to say more. When the speech is done, you do not need to elaborate. If your audience needs something clarified, they will let you know.

Do not forget that overcommunicating can be as annoying and detrimental to a relationship as can under communicating. This is why it is important to empathize with your audience and be able to find balance.

In business settings, it is important to have meetings about things, some that are for planning for future events, and some that are to inform about something already decided. Either way, the meeting should have an agenda and follow it. This way, it does not run overly long, and points are neither forgotten nor does time run out.

Be respectful of other's time in a meeting. If just a few of you go off on a tangent or speak in-depth about something that the rest of the group is not working on and does not impact the reason for the meeting, suggest this be taken offline.

In closing, if you need to call a colleague about something, be sensitive to their situation. If they do not have time to socialize, notice their haste. They will do their best to answer your question, but let them off the hook, saying you will catch up with them later.

CHAPTER 3

ART OF LISTENING

They say you have two ears and one mouth. This means what you hear is more valuable than what you say. This is because you can only speak well about things that you know about.

You cannot say the right things if you do not know what you're talking about. Here we talk about listening and how it goes deeper than just hearing someone talk.

When you are in an unfamiliar group or situation, you might feel like you need to make a strong impression upon the people there in order to be accepted. However, this almost invariably backfires. When you are trying too hard, it shows.

Have you ever heard the saying that when you are in Rome, you should do as the Romans do? This means when you are the new person in a group of people, the best way to endear yourself to them is to get a feel for who they are and how they operate. Ask them questions about themselves. People enjoy talking about themselves, and they will also appreciate that you were considerate enough to think about them.

Listen to them and face them when they are speaking to you. Put away your cell phone and engaged, undistracted. At this moment, be present, even if you hear other conversations or what is going on at another table. When you are in the moment during a conversation, you are giving the impression that the person you are speaking with is important and that you care about what they have to say.

Do not jump in and talk over the other person. For one thing, you need to listen to their point fully because if you jump in before you have heard the other's position. This will help you avoid speculating incorrectly and causing a misunderstanding. Reserve judgment, if you jump to a conclusion, you actively disengage from the conversation.

Have you ever gotten to a point in a conversation that you know what the other person is going to say? Abstain from doing this because even if you think you know what will be said next, it flies in the face of good listening skills. You do not know exactly what someone else is going to say. Instead of engaging in this poor habit, instead, visualize what is being said. This will be received by the other person far better. Ask them if you can help them with anything. This shows initiative and a desire to contribute to the group.

A conversation is a two-way street, so, of course, you should ask questions that help you bring the point a little more in focus. I'm sure you have heard it before, and I'll reinforce the fact that paraphrasing what the other has said is a great tool because if you have something wrong, you can then be enlightened. During this, you may even get further details that will help you understand.

During conversations, there may be pauses. That is okay. It gives time to reflect and enjoy the time talking. Silence does not have to be awkward. Absent body language and energy such as crossed arms, sour expressions, and pointing the body away from you, is a problem. Think about what has been said while you take in the atmosphere. Are you outside with a cool breeze? Smile at the other person, and they will likely mirror your expression.

Be sure you are really listening so that if you are asked a question, you will not be embarrassed. Do not let your mind wander off thinking about something else.

Try not to get stuck on a small piece you may not agree with so that you close yourself off and stop listening. They say, "Don't sweat the small stuff," so keep your mind and heart open to the conversation at hand. Let the person get their point across and then address your concerns.

Make it an open dialog and veer away from shaming. Your point should be gaining a better understanding. Keep your biases in check because focusing on them will start an internal dialog and stop you from listening. The reason is, your posture changes, and you can start waiting to talk instead of taking anything in. If you keep listening, you may learn that your concern is addressed in the next statement.

Notice your own body, are you sitting comfortably? Relax your shoulders, and try not to fidget. Nobody can absorb knowledge when they are tense because they are focused internally. Also, it is hard to savor an experience with strain on the brain. Practice empathy for the speaker since they may be expressing to you something you would not have thought about because you have not been in their unique circumstance.

Finally, let the conversation change subjects naturally. If you divert attention to another subject before the speaker feels heard, you could do a disservice to the relationship.

CHAPTER 4

HOW TO MANAGE PEOPLE'S ATTENTION

It goes without saying that you need to know how to hold a person's attention if you are going to communicate well with them. Obviously, you cannot just demand to be listened to. The most important thing when learning how to keep people's attention is to be able to tell when you are losing it.

Let's say you are giving a speech. Take a look at the crowd in front of you. Are they looking at the clock? Are they whispering to one another? Do you notice that no one has asked you a question in a while? These are obvious signals that you have lost your audience. Do not worry; all hope is not lost. You can get them back.

The first thing you need to do is change the subject. Perhaps you have been talking about the one you are currently on for too long. Another thing that might be going wrong is that you are not convincing them why they should listen. You might have a speech that is packed with great information, but how does it affect your audience? Why should they take action? How will this affect their lives? If your subject is conserving the rainforest, you need to make your audience understand that the security of the rainforest is in their best interest. Make it relatable to them.

Another way to keep your audience's attention is to incorporate a story into your speech. Say you are a math professor. If you just show your students a bunch of calculations and formulas written on a whiteboard, you will not grip them. However, if you tell a story about a real-life situation where this knowledge helped you, they will then infer that they could find value in it. Letting them know how the formulas they learn and the equations they practice will be used in the real world can capture the attention of more students, those who are less interested in math for math's sake.

It is important to understand the human attention span. What I am about to say is not to be insensitive or to invalidate your interests. It is merely to be realistic. For everyone, their own lives are naturally going to be the most interesting stories for us. It is not a bad trait. Everyone is self-interested, and that is the way it should be. Therefore, there are certain things we could talk about for hours that would not catch the interest of other people. You might feel like taking the people around you through the entire night when you went to your favorite artist's concert, but they do not have that emotional connection to that night. There is no way they could; they were not there. This is not their favorite artist.

One thing that will never work in getting people's attention when you are losing it is to talk harder at them, hoping that will get them to shift their focus back to you. This never works. In fact, it could cause them to tune you out more.

Engaging your audience is super important. Take them on a journey as you talk to them. Move them through a time-line with checkpoints. Ask questions of your audience either collectively asking them all to answer at once, or by calling on someone specific. Humor about situations that everyone can relate to even though it is unpleasant keeps people alert. Let's say that you are encouraging people to start an exercise program. You may use the analogy that it is just impossible to get up out of bed, and you can go through how you hit the snooze button like five times, and now you do not have the time you need to do your whole workout. Everyone knows that feeling of not wanting to get up. People will have a good laugh, and you will have connected with them on a fundamental level.

Speakers need to have a point and get to that point. Listeners are more likely to experience loss of focus if they feel that you are ambling about without a place to get to. Everyone's attention span has a limit. Make sure you remember than when preparing to speak. If you are talking to small children, their attention span is lower than a full-grown adult.

Another very important and extremely useful tool to use in speaking to people is to pull on the heartstrings. The well-loved 13th Episode of Season 1 of the TV Series "Madmen," about the climate of Advertising Agencies in the 1960s, Season 1 Episode 13, depicts this idea effectively when the main character Don Draper pitches an idea for the Carousel product for Kodak. The client wanted to call it a wheel. However, Don Draper invoked very strong emotion by referring to the root meaning of the word "nostalgia" and that in Greek, the word meant "pain from an old wound." He referred to the product as a time machine, taking you back to a place you longed to go again and ideating that looking at your old photos with this product can let a person travel the way a child does.

Tapping into something your audience will care about is a great way to hold their attention.

CHAPTER 5

BEING SEEN, HEARD AND UNDERSTOOD

To communicate effectively, you must have the ability to get others to understand what you are saying. This might sound like an obvious statement, but there is a lot that goes into it, and not just with the words you say. You must manage how you say it and whether your body language backs it up.

So often, it is less about the message and more about how you give it. Here you will find out how to express your ideas in a way that is palatable to others, and how to adjust to the modern way of communication.

First, you need to know your audience. There are a few factors that go into this. For one, you need to make sure your speech is age-appropriate. You would not go to a kindergarten classroom and say something like, "It would appear that there has been a misconception about…" etc. They would not understand what you were saying, and the delivery of your speech would leave them confused and bored. Tailor your verbiage to those listening to you.

The first communication blocker we are going to talk about is using placeholders such as "like" or "you know." If used to often, it can make it difficult for others to follow your sentences because it gets in the way of your message.

Whenever you feel like you are going to use one of these words, just pause for a moment and think about what you are going to say next. It will go over much better. Soon, you will need to pause

less until this habit is no longer a part of your speech.
Sometimes people are not understood because they do not directly say what they are feeling, and instead use cryptic messages.

It is not rude to ask for exactly what you want. In fact, it is saving yourself trouble as well as others. You will no longer have to deal with feelings of frustration because you do not feel like you are being heard.

It is as simple as it sounds. When you want something, request it. Be specific. For example, you are in the car with your friend, and they ask you where you want to eat. You feel like having tacos. Say straight out, "I'd like to go to the place that makes such good tacos." This will leave no room for doubt about what you want.

Your first impression begins when you first walk into the room. This is why you need to watch your body language because you can turn people away just from nonverbal cues. The most common example is folding your arms. When your arms are crossed in front of your chest, this is a defensive position. It is telling others that you want to be left alone. In addition, it is a means of minimizing yourself. Do not be afraid to take up space around you. Of course, this means also making sure not to encroach upon the personal space of others, but rest your arms comfortably if you are sitting down. Keep your shoulders back. Posture is everything in communication. It is sometimes the things you do not say out loud that send the clearest message.
Another thing you must learn is that appearances do matter. The way you dress has an impact on both how you are seen and how you behave. That might sound strange, but think about this. When you just want to stay at home and watch movies, the way you dress will show this. You will be wearing clothes to lounge comfortably in. Therefore, when you go to a business situation dressed too casually, you will not be setting yourself up to take the event seriously. It will then be easier to slouch over or wander off. Your language will also be less business-like. This is why the term "look good, feel good" exists. Think about when you are

dressed up nice, and you know it. When you pass people in the halls, they tell you that you look nice. This causes you to be much more confident in how you act and speak. The people who win people over are the ones who are comfortable in their own skin and confident enough to speak out in front of others. This means you must build yourself up to be this way.

When you are having a conversation with someone, make sure your body language is open to the other person. This will make them feel like what they are saying is important to you.

When speaking, volume and tone is the key. You need to make your voice audible, but keep it from being overwhelming. An overly loud voice will cause people to distance themselves from your voice. If you talk too quietly, others will not be able to hear you, but it can also be off-putting. They might mistake you for being shy or timid.

Being seen, heard, and understood is not about making a spectacle of yourself. It is about saying what you mean with conviction and not being afraid to be noticed.

CHAPTER 6

CHARISMATIC COMMUNICATION

The concept of empathy is one that is often misunderstood. Empathy is sometimes viewed as a sign of being a pushover. Seeing the other side of things does not mean you changed your mind. It just means you understand where that person is coming from. It is the ability to walk a mile in another's shoes.

Let's say a father finds out his son talked rudely to their teacher at school. They also know that their child is under a lot of stress because of an illness in the family. If the father gave his son no consequences and told him it was alright because of what he was going through, that would make him an enabler. However, let's say the offense would normally earn the son being grounded for a week, but because of the extenuating circumstances, the father decides to shorten the grounding for three days along with being required to write a letter of apology to his teacher. The father would be showing empathy there because he realizes his son was not in his right mind and that this outburst was the result of stress rather than actual malice. However, it also impacts his son's ability to be empathetic, by driving home that he cannot use life events as a crutch to get away with bad behavior.

Another common assumption is that empathy is the same thing as pitying a person. When you empathize with someone, you consider how the things they are going through might make them feel. Imagine seeing someone trip over and fall. You would think back to a time this had happened to you. You would conjure up the physical pain and emotional embarrassment that comes with it. This will make you able to be more effective in your dealings with them because you will know what they need to feel better. It is also often wrongly assumed that you cannot build up empathy. While there are people who lack the ability to feel for others, I can already tell that you are not one of them. If you were, you would never have bothered to pick up a book about empathy. You can foster empathy and build it up.

The basis of empathy is curiosity. When we make assumptions about a person or thing, we do not consult them in the process of making our judgments about them. That process happens internally, and we use our set of beliefs and specific experiences often without their knowledge. It is our empathy that helps us relate to others.

You can disagree with someone's actions and still have empathy for them because you can understand what causes them to do the things they do. For example, when someone has an unpleasant personality, this behavior tends to be motivated by negative experiences and wrong teachings during childhood. Say you have a coworker who acts cold towards others and responds to people with short, sharp answers. As you learn about their life, you learn that their spouse is going through a grave illness.

This makes you realize that this person might not always even realize that they are being rude or realize how short their fuse is because they are just acting out what they are taught. This knowledge would help you interact with them in the most productive possible way.

Empathy does not mean absolving someone, although when you can understand where others were coming from when they make poor decisions, you can see the difference between someone who is truly reprehensible and a person who was in a bad position. No one is above this, and it could happen at any age. If you want others to be understanding when you make mistakes, you cannot withhold that same gesture from them.
We pay for our latitude with our tolerance.

Any time you are trying to sell a product, you need to utilize empathy because knowing what sells means digging into the psychology of another person. You learn what impassions them and what motivates them to consider one brand over another.

Empathy is not a weakness. It is something that will make you powerful; you will understand the way the mind works. You will see yourself become business-savvy and watch your social skills improve dramatically.

Empathy is a necessary quality of leadership because a manager needs to understand his/her people fundamentally. S/he needs to know what motivates them, and what demotivates them along with what makes them strong down to what their derailers are and why they have them.

Ultimately, having empathy for someone does not mean you need to solve their problems. You can offer small gestures that make them feel good and let them know that you can see things from their perspective without having an internal struggle about how to fix things. Empathy allows you to give another person the comfort of knowing that they are understood. It costs nothing to let someone know you are trying to understand how they feel and that you regard them with kindness.

You already have the basics of empathy. However, you are capable of training yourself to have an even stronger sense of it. To increase your empathy, you must be able to see from the point of view of another person even if they are completely different from you. This does not mean you have to cross over and become one of them. It just means you see where you might be able to relate to them. Even within our differences, there are still similarities. When you are learning about a lifestyle that is different from yours, you can still get a sense of how they could feel about the things that are important to their culture. This could cause you to think of the things that are a significant part of your lifestyle. When you conjure up the feelings that come from these artifacts, rituals, or ceremonies, transfer those feelings to the other person.

When therapists establish empathy for their clients, they often mirror what the patient says. This is not a word-for-word parroting of it, but a summarization. For example, a patient comes in and says they are struggling with meeting the demands of their strict parents. Suppose your patient talks about how their parents expect them to get straight A's while being involved in multiple extra-curricular activities, all while volunteering on the weekends. The therapist tells them, "I gather that you feel overwhelmed by your workload." This may seem obvious, but the therapist is trying to let the patient know they understand their situation.

Our interactions with other people will be more beneficial to both them and us when we are able to connect with them on an emotional level. Try this exercise. Next time you watch your favorite show, try to switch positions with your favorite character and their enemy. When we have biases built up, it can cause us to think a person could do no wrong, or not consider the idea that they might be right. While this is harmless when you think about a TV show, it is easy to pull this concept into real life. In this exercise, actively work at seeing the situation in favor of the other character. As you do this, you will probably start to see moments where your preferred character does not shine so brightly, and the one you have disliked might actually have substantial grievances with them. For example, you might realize their anger, while expressed poorly, came about because the other character caused them to get in trouble at work and therefore miss out on the promotion they had worked hard for.

Empathy is not just a feeling for someone during tough times. In fact, that is much easier than it is to feel happy for someone when they have gotten something you would like to have. You are not going to avoid feeling a little jealousy, but you have to make sure this is a fleeting emotion because it gets in the way of your ability to connect with your empathy. For example, your friend gets engaged, and your partner has not brought up marriage yet. It is only natural to have that fact go through your mind, but you also need to remember that just because you are not engaged now, does not mean it will not happen. Also, think about what your friend has been through to get to this point. They might have had very negative experiences in relationships before their current one. With this in mind, you can realize how much they have needed this to happen. When we are jealous, it prevents us from thinking about other people.

Some people claim to be an "empath" because people often tell them very personal things, but in reality, they are the opposite. They were asking very personal questions, which led the person to tell very revealing information. A true empath is someone who waits until the other person is comfortable sharing information with them, and they do not bait them into doing so. At this point, you might be wondering what the right thing to say is. This is actually not as important as the atmosphere you create for the person. Sometimes the assurance is nonverbal. You can give them a hug or put your hand on their shoulder. Sometimes it is about keeping eye contact with them, which lets them know you are really listening to them, which is often at the heart of what people want when they are sharing a problem with you. Keeping it bottled inside is hurting them, and they need to vent to someone so they can look at their problem with clarity and figure out what they are going to do. Remember that properly expressing empathy for the person does not mean you need to know exactly what to say. It just means you are there in the moment with them, no matter what that means.

When great speakers are mentioned, there is always talk of their charisma. They have something that just pulls you, and you cannot stop watching and listening to them. What exactly does that mean? When we hear that word, it is easy to think that means a "larger than life" persona, and we conjure up images of celebrities and public figures. You may think of Martin Luther King, whose work on civil rights and rousing speeches are heralded even today as being the most moving of all time. Bill Clinton, 42nd President of the United States of America, has a way of making you think he is speaking directly to you and only you. He created an environment of explosive economic growth that was unprecedented, resulting in a budget surplus of $236B. Media mogul and philanthropist, Oprah Winfrey, speaks with an earnestness such that her audience feels as though she truly understands their plight. She has a generosity of spirit that cannot be ignored.

They usually have such polish and instinctive know-how, with their body language, to command attention. They always look perfect and seem to never make the daily mistakes everyone else does. This makes them seem unapproachable, and the thought of meeting them makes you nervous.

Even a profoundly flawed person capable of evil deeds can have charisma. Adolf Hitler, the leader of the Nazi party and a dictator of enormous power, was able to use his own charisma to capture the ear of people experiencing devastating economic problems and political unrest to build one of the most destructive forces of the 20th century resulting in the invasion of 22 countries across Europe and the murder of over 6 million innocent people.

Charisma inspires people to believe in someone, make them interested in subjects that had previously been apathetic about. When someone has mastered this art, people want to get close to them. They feel like they can relate to this person. No one wants to watch someone who is perched upon a platform and talking down to them. This means your number one goal when speaking to others in any form is to form a connection with them. Think about those ads you see on the TV that are trying to sell a certain type of soda. It shows a montage of a group of friends spending time together while drinking this soda. This is designed to make you imagine doing similar things with the people in your life.

To be relatable, you have to know your strengths and make them the most visible qualities. When you try to present yourself as someone other than who you are, people will pick up on it.

Charisma is certainly a gift, but it can be practiced and accessed by a person who does not believe they have that quality. First, charismatic people exude confidence and energy. They are not tired and dull and seem to have all the time in the world. They may put a lot of thought into what they wear. As the saying goes, "dress for the job you want."

It is the small things that matter in communication. Tiny non-verbal gestures may be communicating things that are contrary to the charismatic image you want to display. Eye contact and facial expression are very important and should be practiced in front of a mirror. The way you break eye contact is important and where you look. Project your energy onto others and get them to talk about themselves, their motivations, and what they really want.

Everyone has their own special personality, and it should shine through as you practice the art of charisma. If you are playful and funny, embrace that as a part of who you are. People enjoy an exciting story or a good laugh. If you are a more cerebral, serious person that can work to your advantage as well. People trust someone slightly reserved with intelligence.

Positive energy is contagious. Have you ever noticed that when you come into a room in a great mood with high energy that it makes people wonder what has the spring in your step? People smile more and laugh easier. By contrast, if you walk into a room with slumped shoulders and a bland expression, people may avoid you?
Charismatic people tend to how present they are in the conversation by turning their whole body towards the person they are speaking to. Their shoulders and feet are pointed towards their audience.

Confidence is an essential element of charisma, and healthy

habits like exercise make you move your body in a more self-assured manner. It also helps the clothing you select to hang on you better. The visual appeal part of charisma cannot be ignored.

Remember to keep your self-talk positive, notice things you did during a conversation that had a good outcome, and reinforce that behavior. Notice things you may have done better, but make improvements to your focus. Enjoy the benefits of practicing charisma and how it can help you to achieve your life goals.

CHAPTER 7

THE POWER WORDS TO USE IN COMMUNICATION

One message can be conveyed in many different ways. Sometimes we have to say things that are difficult but necessary. While you cannot be afraid to make criticisms when you are in a leadership position, there is a right and wrong way to go about it. You must say it in a way that they can absorb. To do this, start out with a compliment. People will be more willing to receive what you have to say about their work whenever you give them some positive feedback. If you do not do this, it will feel like a beatdown for them, and they will feel less motivated in the future. Instead of just telling the person they did something incorrectly, offer them a suggestion of what they could do differently in the future. Give them a guideline. Offer future improvements.

In your personal relationships, no matter how much you like the person, there are going to be times where they annoy or frustrate you. It does no good to bottle these things up, so the question becomes how to let them be known in a way that helps the relationship instead of harming it. A key word in this situation is "we."

Even the most thick-skinned people have a hard time hearing that they have done something that is upsetting someone we care about. There is a pride factor; no one likes being called out. There is fear involved. Hearing that the person is upset with you will make you worry about the state of your relationship.

Let's say you do not like the fact they interrupt you when you are speaking. If you said, "you always interrupt me," this would put them in a defensive position. Instead, try telling them something like, "I think our relationship would be stronger if we let each other finish our sentences." This would send them the message, but not in a way that places blame onto them or makes them feel like they are inferior because your goal is not to let them know they did something wrong. It is to teach them how to do something right.

When you are trying to deliver a message to someone, the most important thing to do is keep your verbiage upbeat and your goal to come to a mutual understanding, making it so that people want to do so with you. You have probably seen those videos where someone is trying to make you see their side on a certain social or political issue. They use words such as "wake up, people" or "your world is falling apart around you, and you don't even know it." Their goal is to stir up a sense of urgency within their audience, but what they really end up doing is frightening them and insulting their intelligence. They do not want to hear this person talk anymore because they have antagonized themselves.

A better persuasive tactic is to offer a solution. Let's say you are trying to sell a type of vacuum cleaner. A good leading statement might be, "did you know you can clean your floors in half the time you usually do? This will add up to a lot of free time!" Here, you have given your audience a vision of a better future with your product. You have not insulted their taste by saying, "Did you know the vacuum you have right now is terrible?" This may sound like a good persuasive tactic, but when you start out on a negative note, you are setting your audience up to become upset with you.

When you disagree with someone, the most powerful words you can say are, "I understand where you are coming from." This might seem strange because you are on opposite sides with this person. However, remember that this does not mean you have to dislike this person or that there is no common ground. The most powerful moments in a debate are when the participants share a thought. This shows both your opponent and others that conflict does not make you disregard others as people. When you give someone that bit of understanding, they will be more prone to hear you out.

Let's say you feel like your partner misses out on family time too much because of work. Do not word this like an attack because it will make them think you do not appreciate their contributions. Tell them, "I know you have a demanding job and that your work helps us out a great deal." Here, you have validated them. You are not standing over them and accusing them of doing something wrong. Sometimes, you never have to word your grievances in a way that makes them seem as such. You might choose to invite them to do something that would alleviate the behavior that is frustrating for you. For example, "would you like to go to the park this weekend, just you, me, and the kids?" Again, employ the "we"- suggest the family as a whole does not look at their phone. Now, you have turned what could have been an argument into a bonding moment that sets a precedence for the future.

CHAPTER 8

WIN PEOPLE TO YOUR WAY: THE POWER OF PERSUASION

Empathy is not only about how you can help other people, even though that is a benefit to it. It can aid you in your own endeavors. Do not worry about using empathy to serve yourself. People who do things for themselves are not bad people. Thinking about your own interests is not a bad thing. You have not only right to do this, but a responsibility. You are the only person who is going to do exactly what is right for you because you are the only one who knows what that is.

If you are going to try to change a person's mind, you need first to find common ground with the person even when they are on the other side. For example, you are trying to create a positive relationship with your best friend's significant other when you have not in the past. What you might tell this person first is that you understand the two of you have had your differences in the past. Offer an apology for any part you played in that. Then remind the person of what you have in common with them, that you both care about your friend. Now you will have their attention. Talk about the fact that you two arguing is hurting this person. They might not have thought about it that way before. Now you are working towards a common goal. You want to make things better for your best friend and their significant other.

When we think about what qualities make a leader, words like "strong" and "unflappable" often come up. While strength is indeed important, you also need something that will make you appealing to those you want to follow you. There is a reason people do not form attachments with the "ice queen" persona. Think about someone you have watched on television who never changed their tone of voice or facial expression, and they never had an emotional reaction to anything, no matter how what the circumstance was. You probably felt indifferent about them because there was nothing to connect to. They never cracked a smile or told a joke, meaning they did not have any quirks that made them stand out. They never showed any vulnerability. There were never any insecurities or flaws for you to relate to. In short, they never did anything to humanize themselves to you.

Think about when a public figure shares a personal struggle they have been through, whether it is about a major life event, stage fright, or anything else of this sort. At that moment, you felt connected to them because it made you think of a time when you faced a challenging situation. Then they will not look at you and feel insecure. In fact, they will be able to draw strength from you when they realize you face challenges but still can strive for great things.

Do not be always feel the need to take yourself seriously. When you make a mistake, laugh it off. Poke a little fun at yourself. This will let others know you do not feel like you are above them. Is there any other time those in a leadership position are loved more than when they do something that shows they are "one of us"? Maybe they get their words jumbled up. Maybe they trip over. When they take it in stride, they create a relatable moment. Winning people over is less about impressing them and more about connecting with them. That is why empathy plays such a large role in leadership skills. Sometimes it shows up in the little things. When you see people that you know, smile, wave, and say hello. It is extremely powerful when you let those you are in a leadership position over know that you see them. This ties back into why the "ice queen" persona does not work. People want to get behind someone who can benefit them, and how would they trust a person to do that if they do not feel like the person even knows what they need. Ask them how they are doing and if there is anything they need help with.

Finally, remember that your goal is to get people to like you, not to create a person you think others will like. If you do the latter, this will be hard to hold up. Accentuate the strengths you already have. Do not write off your sense of humor as being unattractive. Perhaps it is exactly what makes you unique and therefore adds appeal to your personality. Give people compliments where they are due. If you think someone's hair looks nice, tell them so. You do not know what impact this might have on someone. They could be having the worst day of their lives, and to hear one person tell them something nice could completely change how they are feeling. They will remember this event, and this will impact how they feel the next time you see them. Kind gestures do not even have to come at your expense, but they can lead to paying off in the future.

To persuade others, you must get into their mindset. Why would they want to think your way? What would be in it for them?

To learn about how to make persuasion work, we will go over tactics that do not.
First and foremost, the harsh language will not work for you in the long run. Here are some examples of that:

- Scare tactics- "If you do not join our cause, something horrible will happen to you."
- Virtue signaling- "If you do not follow me, you are not on the right side."
- Condemning- "If you do not donate to us, something terrible will happen to people or animals, and you will be complicit."
- Emotional manipulation- "You do care about the less fortunate, don't you?"

While these tactics might get you a couple of easy victories, over time, they will have negative consequences for your reputation.

You do not want to be seen as a manipulator. It will make people question the integrity of your cause. You have probably heard of organizations that accepted donations, claiming to give them to a cause. Many people are passionate about this, and then the organization turns out to be using this money dishonestly.

Manipulation is also a sign of insecurity. It suggests that you do not have faith in your ability to influence, so you need to resort to underhanded methods. The goal of persuasion is to give a person actively and openly or group a different perspective. You are advising them, which gives them the sense that you have their best interest at heart.
The basic difference between true persuasion and manipulation is that in persuasion, you are not trying to hide the fact that you aim to influence their thoughts. There is no guise of standing for a higher moral cause.

Before you try to change a person's opinion, you must show respect for theirs. This is why you need to leave out things such as "everything you ever believed is wrong." This statement puts people on edge right off the bat.

Imagine a teacher trying to convince their class to spend some time reading over their summer vacation. If they said "video games will turn your brain to mush," they would lose the attention of their audience because they would interpret that they are trying to portray their favorite activities as bad. A better approach would be, "I want you to have fun this summer, but you should also take a few minutes each day to brush up on your reading skills." From there, the teacher could launch a discussion about the mental health benefits that come from reading. Of course, it would be alright to list health conditions that reading could help prevent. It is an effective persuasion tactic to let the audience know how following your suggestion could protect them. Following this, she could suggest a reading list to her students. Here, she includes books of all genres that are age-appropriate and tailored to what her students might be interested in.

Now, she has presented her idea as one that would be beneficial to her student's lives and has given them a reason they should listen to her.

Make sure you know all of your facts before you speak. This will have the automatic effect of making your demeanor appear confident. It will also prepare you for any potential questions your listener could have. Speak with conviction and do not doubt yourself.

Remove words like "maybe" and "I guess" from your vocabulary. Rather, only use them when there is truly no evidence that supports one definite conclusion. Otherwise, you will appear unsure of yourself. If you are not sure of yourself, why should anyone else trust you? For this reason, people who struggle with a stutter or other speech impediment are encouraged to seek help in correcting this issue. If you do this, you will find that your speeches are better received because you will present your information from a place of affirmativeness.

Remember that your goal is not to win everyone over, as that is impossible. If someone completely disagrees with you and does not want to hear anything you have to say, understand that you are dealing with a lost cause and move on. This isn't being a quitter. Rather it is knowing a sound investment of time, which is a skill any effective leader must-have.

Finally, give your audience something that they are working for. People need to feel like what they are doing means something. If you want people to help your cause, you must show them results for their efforts. For example, an animal shelter who wants volunteers and donations cannot only show people animals that are in bad shape. This will make them think nothing is being done. However, if you show donors a picture of an animal they helped save moving into their forever home, they will be assured that their efforts were worth something. This will also increase your credibility because it is proof of you getting something accomplished.

Effective persuasion is not about being a charmer or "talking the talk." It is about coming from a genuine place, giving potential followers benefits for their efforts, and showing that you can back up what you say you are going to do.

CHAPTER 9

BOOST ENTHUSIASM AMONG YOUR COLLEAGUES

We all work because we need to make money. While everyone wants to be incented correctly in terms of money, but real enthusiasm in the workplace can only be achieved when your workplace represents some things that transcend money and motivates you on a much deeper level.

Companies have mission statements to give employees, customers, and partners a clear idea of what they stand for. For example, Coca-Cola's mission statement is, "To refresh the world... To inspire moments of optimism and happiness... To create value and make a difference.". This is inspiring and conjures up lots of warm feelings, and you can almost see that old 1971 Coca-Cola commercial with people of all colors singing "I'd Like to Teach the World to Sing," and we are taken back to a simpler time where all of the world's problems can be solved with a refreshing drink.

This is the way companies try to encourage staff and bring them together.
There are things you can do personally to motivate your colleagues and create a better atmosphere in your workplace. They say one candle loses nothing by lighting another candle, and it is true. When someone on your team does something well, and you think it is best-in-class, tell them, let them know, and copy their direct managers. Nothing is more motivating than to have the quality of your work recognized. It is also an empathetic response to lift up someone else's work. Just as you enjoy it when

someone gives you an "attaboy," and it spurs you on towards better performance, others will react in a like manner.

By the same token, when you see a colleague doing a task in a way that causes him/her extra work, and you know a way that will help them get a better result quicker, tactfully let them know. Train them and give them the tools they need to improve their job performance. A sense of empathy will allow you to do this without embarrassing them. Done right, you can advocate for a sharing of information between your colleagues, and this will make for a very enthusiastic, motivated place of work.

By the same token, if there are people in the workplace who are negative and impact productivity and relationships in a way that is not positive, they are detrimental to the mission statement. No one likes to work with a micromanager. With an empathetic heart, you might understand that she is a first-time manager. She does not have a great deal of experience in delegating to or leading people. She is worried that her team will not be productive, and she will not succeed in a leadership role. Let her know by word and by deed that she can count on you, and she will very likely begin to have faith in you and loosen the reigns so you can do your job more effectively. If things persist, and she is not showing the leadership qualities that management gave her credit for, talk to someone in human resources. Often, with some management coaching from a mentor in the company and continued support from you, she will relax into her role and be able to manage more effectively.

The point is to be the change you want to see in your workplace. Do you want people to be more open? Then be more open about obstacles you are having, ways that you have found to do the job more effectively, and about successes you have seen with respect to your colleagues.

Do you hear complaints from colleagues? Some of this might be just about personalities, however, boil it down. Do you hear actual grievances that can be addressed? If so, you can describe it dispassionately and offer solutions. You can make a change in your company. For example, if you learn that management does not listen to its employees, you can facilitate a conversation between management and employees to learn from each other and find ways to operate in a way that more closely resembles the company mission statement.

What I'm saying is that you can move away from the victim mentality of accepting that things will not change and you cannot be an agent of change. You can make a difference. This can be in each aspect of your professional life.

In addition to your colleagues and internally within your company, boost enthusiasm in dealing with your clients and customers. When your customers feel heard and empathized with, your company will have a better chance of getting their loyalty and future business. Your customers deserve to hear an enthusiastic voice during their touchpoints in your company. This includes the salesperson who creates the relationship with them, to the customer service representative who answers the phone when they have a problem.

You would be surprised how a little kindness can go a long way in the workplace can boost enthusiasm. This can be anything from remembering a birthday to bringing donuts one morning, to noticing a colleague has a cough and offering them cough drops. One of my most memorable acts of kindness someone has done for me at work was to have a place setting at my desk when I came in for work, and I was told that was my invitation to lunch in celebration of a new apartment. The colleague had made ham and potato salad. This type of thing certainly increases amicable relationships and a passion or zeal for work.

Do what you can to build a rapport with colleagues, and you will be repaid with a better work environment.

CHAPTER 10

HOW TO ANTICIPATE OBJECTIONS AND MANAGE RELATIONSHIP RULES

One of the most important aspects of leadership is learning how to handle criticism gracefully. We live in a world where everyone will make their own judgments on people and things and put them out on social media for the whole world to see and comment on. This means you will never be able to win everyone's favor. The first step of anticipating objections is to know that they will inevitably come your way any time you put yourself out there in any public way.

You need to know that you do not have to convince everyone to think your way. Think about any website that supports videos uploaded by users. Underneath each video, you will find an option to like or dislike it. No matter how many likes a video has, there will also be dislikes, and the opposite is true. There are mixed views about everything. You will gain power when you come to realize that.

First, thank the person for taking the time to review your work. This may not be your first instinct because it is hurtful to receive criticism. However, this will show maturity within you. Just because you do this, does not mean that you have to take their suggestions, but acknowledging it is a positive act. Encourage them to create too, bearing in mind that what they want to see in your work, they can do on their own. A candle does not lose light by lighting another. Keep in mind that you do not have to insult the other person to defend yourself.

Another thing to remember is that you do not need to respond to each piece of criticism you receive. If you are being met with baseless accusations or the person is obviously just trying to be hurtful by name-calling, insults, etc., the best thing to do is ignore this person.

No matter what career you chose, you will need to learn to anticipate and overcome objections because at the basis of every function lies an element of salesmanship. Experience helps you think on your feet in a more agile fashion because even as you think of many types of objections that could come up, you can still be surprised. Your best first step is to be positive and inquisitive. Ask questions about the objection that will help you to understand the other person's thinking. Avoid interrupting the other person, let them express themselves entirely. When you do, you develop solutions and counter-arguments.

Some of the objections you anticipate are pretty obvious to you, such as price. In this economic climate, everyone is quite budget-conscious, and they want to maximize the impact they get for the money they spend. Most want a little something extra to feel like they have gotten a deal.

Anticipating objections is something we learn even as we grow up and ask our parents for privileges such as staying out an extra hour or for a sleepover party. Often, you may have offered to do extra chores or help babysit siblings or promising not to ask for anything again for a long time.

A spouse wanting to go on a fishing trip with friends will likely agree to a honey-do list of chores to finish before the trip, or perhaps they consent to purchase a new appliance that will be going on sale next month.

Often, when pitching an idea to someone, the objection is about timing. Perhaps they do not feel ready to make a decision. Everyone knows what it is like to be in the shop and compare mode when a salesperson comes and starts to pitch us. They give us information about various brands and their own opinions. Soon, they will see that we may not be ready to make the purchase, and they will try to overcome the situation by understanding the reason for it. If they sense that you are not convinced about the quality of the item, they will start to give statistics and things they have heard from other clients. If the timing is about money, the salesperson may be able to offer a zero percent interest card for a period of time. This way, if you pay it off before-hand, then you will not pay extra for interest, this is ideal.

S/he will likely go the extra mile to be seen as trustworthy by you. It is actually more important to instill trust than it is to be informative. For example, the salesperson may tell you some negative reviews about a product and say that they rather have you be happy with a product and feel good about buying from them than to make a sale today.
This is a very powerful language and implies that your faith in them is more important than their own commission. Do you notice that this action puts you immediately at ease?

The best way to anticipate objections is to pretend you are the customer. What would be important to you, and what things would be barriers for you to create an agreement?

Do you believe your relationships are all they could be? Are you experiencing friction too often? Do you find that your conversations with family and friends tend to cycle through the same points of contention and do not move forward and get better? If you are experiencing difficulty in getting to a place of understanding in your relationships, you may need to brush up on the level of empathy you are approaching your interpersonal relationships with.

Empathy can help you concerning your professional life with your career as well. Whether you are a salesperson wanting to maximize your sales, or a human resources leader wanting to mediate between different departments, functions, or employees, the ability to understand how someone feels will help you succeed. For example, empathy helps the salesperson be able to get a client to open up about what keeps them up at night and, as every good salesperson knows, if you can identify and solve a problem, you can make a sale. The human resources associate who can empathize will have no issue working through a dispute in the workplace or bringing into focus the profile of the right candidate for a job. In every aspect of a business, no matter what function you are in, it can be said that you have clients, both external and internal. Your internal clients are those who you report to and those who you do work for. You should approach these individuals from a perspective of customer service.

Have you ever been called upon to run a training session at work? When people are learning something new, they are in a vulnerable position and in order to get them to open themselves up to the training process and more fully embrace your instructions, you need to understand their emotions, be it fear of a new process or system down to their ability to catch on quickly enough.

Empathy is definitely a necessary element if you try to convince your significant other to agree to make a big purchase, or harder still, to relocate for a better job. People tend to dig in their heels if they do not believe they are being heard. If you are trying to get their buy in to purchase a boat, you may come to the conversation with a mental list of the benefits of boat ownership and answers to shoot down any potential arguments against it. Remember, your conversations with your significant other are not debates. You need to allow them time to express themselves, and you need to truly listen because you want the right outcome to enhance your relationship. Listen to their objections because it may reign you in should your aspirations in boat ownership be leaning towards one that is too pricey or renting a boat might make the most sense because of the number of days per month you are likely to be able to take it out on the lake.

The point is, when you keep yourself open to different perspectives, you are increasing your knowledge about people you hold interpersonal relationships with. Trust me, they will appreciate this, and it will boost the trust and intimacy you have with them.

Alternately, if you wait to talk and refuse to see their point of view, they will emotionally constrict and, in return, be too busy defending their perspective to explore yours and vice versa fully. At this moment, your relationship has an opportunity to deepen, but rigidity is a strong deterrent to that. The ability to remain flexible and operate from a place of empathy makes you easier to be honest with.

One example could be if you are a coach for a ball team, you need to be able to motivate a group of people to work together. Each of them has his/her own specific personal circumstances as well as their own physical and emotional state of being. So being present in your conversations with the team both collectively and as individuals will be instrumental in your ability to lead them to victory. As you learn more about your team members, you will learn what motivates them most effectively to work harder so you can better predict how they respond to certain situations. Isn't that powerful?

Everyone wants others to be able to see things their way, and you will have a better chance of getting them to if you can and will return the favor. Some good guidelines to use that will ensure you are open and empathetic is to listen to the other party and absorb what they are saying. Do not dismiss their position because it is different from your own.

Not only will the empathetic approach help you in your relationships with people who are already in your life, but it will also help you when you are meeting new people. Opening ourselves to other's perspectives helps us make new friends as well as in every other instance in which we have human interaction down to when you are in a restaurant and talking with your server. A little empathy can make people want to overachieve for you. Notice the person who is rude to their waiter. They will be avoided and given the bare minimum because the server soon realizes that these are not people who will be pleased. On the other hand, the person who understands when the server is super busy and remains calm will likely get a little extra attention.

In summary, a little kindness and understanding will support you in every interaction with people. Empathy helps you in every aspect of your interpersonal relations and improve your personal life, work relationships, and community.

CHAPTER 11

MAKE FRIENDS QUICKLY AND EASILY

Making friends is so important in everything we do, and friends make life much easier. Friends in the workplace who support each other and are our confidants, you can partner together to build a better work environment. If we need to learn something, friends on the job can teach one another and can vouch for one another should the need arise.

We have friends in our personal lives, such as neighbors and classmates. Making friends with neighbors is so important because you live next to one another. You can watch out for one another and let the other know if they see someone snooping around as well as helping one another in times of need as only a neighbor can. If your neighbor broke a leg and could not mow his lawn, you would surely help him out. Just the same as if you are having a party, and your neighbor would be okay with having extra cars around for an evening. If you have children near the same age, both of you may need occasional help with babysitting or rides.

Friendships do not have to be close to be enriching, you can have a friend who you only see on the train in the mornings, but it's cordial and starts your day off with a nice conversation.

Let's talk about how we make friends and the role that empathy plays in it. We make friends when we interact with others, giving them our time and attention. We look at each other when we talk and spend time listening to them. Most people love it when you remember something about them. The empathetic friend will resist the urge to engage in judgment. Not only that but if a friend opens up to you, they may not be looking for you to problem-solve for them. They may just need a friendly ear.

If you want to make friends with more people, broaden your field of vision when you are out. You never know when an opportunity arises that you can make a new friend. Notice people. Do you see someone in need of assistance? Maybe they are struggling trying to carry something. If you have the time, give them a hand. Strike up a conversation along the way. The way you present yourself is important, so smile and be present during the conversation instead of checking your phone and letting your thoughts race ahead to the next thing you need to do.

Engage in activities that will put you in front of new people. If you are interested in learning to cook, take a class and when your instructor puts you in teams, talk about more than just the task at hand. Ask questions about why they were interested in cooking and what they intend to do to practice. What if the two of you could get together and entertain your families. You can treat them to delicacies you are learning to cook, as well as letting in some practice time for your class.

When we allow ourselves to become self-absorbed and put on blinders when we are out, with a sour look on our faces, we are missing opportunities to make new friends. If you catch yourself doing this, all is not lost. Look the other person in the eyes, and soften your face as well as your voice and apologize. Most people have had a bad day before, and your action will very likely be accepted with empathy. Open up about what has your nerves on edge, and you can literally turn the situation around and make a new friend.

By the same token, unless you think the person could be a danger, try to turn the situation around if someone is cranky. Use a little empathy for them and ask about them. You might learn about them, make a new friend, and help someone through a difficult time.

There are many ways to look at a situation, and every person sees things from a different perspective. By striving to be open to another perspective, you can open your mind to different ways of thinking. Let go of your biases, and you may either have a change of heart about some things or at least learn why people think a certain way. You do not have to agree with someone about everything to be friends with them.

The empathetic response is to make sure they feel as though you have attempted to understand their position. Be sure not to dismiss their feelings. You do not have to convince others to accept your point of view. Understanding their perspective does not require you to change your mind.

When someone tells you about a problem they are having, listen to, and they are worried about their child, who is having trouble with a math class. You need to acknowledge their feelings about the situation. Remember, they are worried about their child. Do not just tell them it will be alright. They have a legitimate fear that their child could fail a class, and that could mean that they have to repeat a grade. Of course, they are worried. Let them express that to you and let them know that they have your support. Importantly, look on the bright side when you are trying to make friends with people. Regard people in a favorable light, and if you see something they do well, say so. People like it when they are complimented and acknowledged for their efforts. That alone will go a long way to help you make friends more quickly.

Interested people are interesting! Show an interest in people when you want to make friends with them. Soon, your calendar will be full of outings and events with new friends.

CHAPTER 12

WHAT MEN WANT AND WOMEN WANT

In these next two chapters, I will discuss the communication differences between men and women, and what this means for how you should approach discussions with them. Keep in mind that when I discuss these things, it is with the knowledge that there are exceptions to the rule, but here, we will go based on how things are generally speaking.
When we think of men's communication style, it is often shorter and to the point. Their main objective with speaking is to pass necessary information. This means there is less use of adjectives and other "flowery language."

The fact of the matter is that men have less interest in keeping up long conversations than women. Once the necessary information has been passed, they are going to lose interest in a shorter amount of time. This means if your target audience is men, you need to curtail your messages. This is when we employ the technique we discussed earlier in the book known as "less is more."

This means if you are advertising a men's product, let it be known how they can use this. Even if it is a hygiene or beauty product, such as hair gel or cologne, use this rule. What will be the end result of them buying this product? What will there be to gain?
This is not to say that men are not at all, driven by emotion. They just express it in different ways. For example, when male friends want to show affection to one another, it might be a pat on the

shoulder or other short nonverbal cues.

When dealing with a crisis, men are more likely to want time to themselves. They will withdraw to do whatever activities they enjoy most. This does not mean they are rejecting you.

When men talk amongst themselves, they probably will not be facing each other. This creates a more casual environment, making them feel more comfortable to speak, which might even make them speak more freely.

Men are more literal with their meaning when they speak. This does not mean they think more simply. It just means they are less likely to use metaphors and beat around the bush when they are communicating. That is why if you are talking to a man and there is a particular issue you would like to address, just say it right out. For example, you think your partner goes out with his friends on weekends too often, and you would like him to spend more time with you. If you do something passive-aggressive like ask, "So, do you want to go to that movie with Bob and Harry?" to try to get him to go to that movie with you instead, you are not likely going to get the results you want. In relationships between men, there is a "no news is good news" climate. If no one explicitly says there is a problem, then they will assume that all is well. Therefore, the more effective way to get what you want would be to ask your partner, "Would you mind if it was just you and me tonight at the movie?" This way, he will know exactly what is on your mind.

Understand that you are placing a lot of pressure on someone when you expect them to know what you want without you telling them what that is. No one is a mind reader, so therefore it is not fair to deem that someone does not care about your needs because they have not picked up on something that you have not expressed. If a behavior bothers you or there is something they have not done that you would like them to, you need to either bring it up in a straightforward way or let it go. Men do not respond well to statements such as "I'm upset with you about something you said last week." They will wonder why you did not say anything a week ago when it happened because their focus tends to be more on the present and future and on the past. When there has been an apology and reconciliation, they will assume there is no more problem, and there needs to be an element of that in a successful relationship. You cannot continue to bring up old problems, or they will never become a part of the past where they can no longer damage the relationship.

Also, remember that nonverbal cues can be either missed or misunderstood. You saying "okay" softly might not register to others as being a sign that you do not like the idea. They might just think you are agreeing. You will not get things you do not ask for. Let's say your partner suggests going out, but you do not feel well. Tell him that specifically. That way, you will not go out feeling unwell and then building up resentment about the fact. We cannot place blame on others for not hearing what we do not say. The takeaway message in communicating with men is to keep it concise and to the point.

Just as women have misconceptions about men's communication, the reverse is true. Of course, to turn the rules entirely in either direction would be unfair. One side would either not feel like they were being heard or like they were being forced to open up even if that made them uncomfortable. This means we must find a way to communicate in a way that adheres to the plights of both sides. However, as a man communicating with a woman, here are some guidelines that will make your interactions with them more successful.

Think about recurring patterns in advertisements for women's products. The aesthetics of the ads have a softer, more ethereal quality. Self-care products come with a list of benefits. You will notice terms like "cleanse your pores," "rich in vitamins," and "exfoliating" will often come up. Notice that these words conjure up feelings of being cleansed and self-improvement. This is because it is important for women. After a long or stressful day, it is common for women to need a bath. This is because the hot water makes them feel relaxed, and it gives the image of washing the day away.

I think it is fair to say that as a general rule, women speak more during the day. This is because they are more likely to share thoughts and feelings. Talking is a bonding activity. Women often prefer to talk to each other while facing the other person. This establishes a connection and assurance that the other person is hearing what they are saying. When talking to women, stay engaged in the conversation.

Earlier, we talked about men's coping mechanisms being more solitary. For women, it is the opposite. They will want to reach out to a friend when they have a problem. This can cause a misfire in communication. Let's say your partner comes to you with a problem at work with her coworker. Your instinct might be to tell her how to fix the problem, which goes on to upset her. She then tells you that you do not want to listen to her. Here is what went wrong. When women open up about personal problems, it is less often that they are seeking an immediate solution. They are trying to get their emotions sorted out about the problem. Listen to what she has to say and reserve judgment. If she asks for your opinion or advice, then it is perfectly alright to make a suggestion, but wait until then.

In communication with women, there is much more use of subtext. You will need to recognize nonverbal cues and what they mean. It does not mean that women are dishonest. It just means that they have a different way of expressing a problem. There will also be times that they feel you out just to make sure there is not a problem. As a man, your partner might ask you questions that make you unsettled at times, such as asking about the state of the relationships. You might be concerned- why is she asking this? Does this mean she is having doubts about being with me? This is not always the case. In fact, she would not be trying to open up a dialogue with you if that was the case. She might just simply be seeking affirmation about your commitment to the relationship. Do not get defensive. Wait until you understand what this conversation is supposed to be about. Women's communication is more nuanced. When women say something, they like to have confirmation that you heard or understand what they just said. Therefore, if you are just nodding, it might be interpreted as you not validating or not having listened.

Women are more interested in the finer details. If she asks you questions about your personal life, hobbies, and whatnot, this means you have a valuable place in her life, and she wants to know about you. Give a clear answer to these questions to give her confirmation that she has an important place in your life as well.

With male friends, there can be long periods without communication. However, the knowledge is still there that the two care for one another. For women, there needs to be the upkeep of contact. If they have not heard from one another in a while, it can cause them to think there is something wrong in the relationship. They worry about drifting apart.

Finally, women are more physically affectionate. These signs, such as hugging, are important to them. It is a sign of connecting with the other person. Of course, we do not want to violate anyone's personal boundaries, but it is also important to uphold that feeling.

The take-home message about communicating with women is that communication needs to be more abundant and more in-depth. It is not always about finding a solution or taking action. It is about building relationships with others, which is important to success in more areas of life than you might think. This is what I want to emphasize. Men are not bad, and neither are women. They both have strengths that others can benefit from.

CHAPTER 13

THE ART OF STORYTELLING: HOW TO TELL STORIES THAT SELL

Maybe you want to write a book. Maybe you want to become a motivational speaker. No matter which form it takes, if you want to make storytelling a large part of your life, you need to know how to connect with others. Before you form your story, you must build a purpose for it. There is an acronym known as PIE used to describe these purposes.

The first one is to persuade. This means you are trying to get your audience to agree with you about a subject.

The second purpose is to inform. This one is straightforward- you are trying to make your audience walk away from your story with the information they did not have before.

The third and final purpose is entertainment. This means you are not trying to convey any message or convince anyone of anything. You just want to tell a story that your audience has fun going through. This purpose is just as important as the other two because we all need a temporary escape from real life sometimes.

If you want a story to sell, the audience or reader needs to be able to relate to it in some way, even if you are not talking about a story that seems far-fetched. Let's say you are telling a fantasy story. You might be excited to tell your audience about the variety of creatures and ancient artifacts in the world you build, and that is good. Still, if you do not add an element that can be related to the real world, it will feel like a bunch of fluff that has no substance. For example, do not be afraid to make your story about a magical kingdom and center it around its monarchs, but go into who these people and the people around them are. Maybe the king has two children, and the younger one feels like their father prefers the older one because he spends more time with them. Now you have placed a relatable story into it. Sibling rivalry is something most people have at least some experience with, and so, therefore, they will empathize with your characters.

Now let's say you want to inform. This does not have to mean your story is boring. Let's say you are telling a historical event to a crowd. It is good to know all of the dates and terms, but make sure you put these details into perspective. You want to hold people's attention. Give them interesting tidbits of interesting information about the historical figures you are talking about. This will make these people more real to your audience. Remember that it does not always have to be about the harsh parts of the event. Talk about friendships. Remind the audience of what these people were fighting to preserve. Throw some positive in there so they will feel a sense of hope and therefore stay interested.

I would go as far as to say the persuasive story is the most difficult one to pull off. This is because the consequences of not doing it successfully are the harshest. Done wrong, and you can come across as demanding or manipulative.

When you persuade, do not try to pull your audience's thoughts to a certain place. Do not ask divisive questions or ones that only allow one acceptable answer. To understand what I mean, think about those social media posts that say "Like and share this post if you love your family. Ignore it if you hate them and do not care what happens to them." That kind of post probably makes you angry.

CHAPTER 14

LAWS OF PERSUASION AND ATTRACTION

When you hear of laws of attraction, you might think of those books that tell you about how to get dates quickly. However, there is a different kind of attractiveness that I want to discuss today.

You have probably heard people being described as having an attractive personality and wonder what that means. One of the first things you will hear is that they make people feel like they are the only person in the world when they are talking to them. This means they listen intently to a person when they are speaking. For example, someone tells you about which college they graduated from. Now would be a good time to ask them what they studied during their time there. It is little gestures like that. When you do this, you are letting them know that you are not just waiting for your next opportunity to talk. You are taking an active interest in them.

It is said that the most attractive thing a person can wear is a smile. This is because when you do this, you come across as a pleasant and cheerful person. Positive people are automatically seen as more attractive people. Think about how you feel around a person who is always in a bad mood and talks about how nothing ever goes right for them. Being around them makes you feel uncomfortable, and it can even drain your energy levels.

Be an uplifting member of your team. Where others see problems, look for solutions. Let's say your company has had a setback due to a crisis going on in the outside world. This is going to be a time where those around you are afraid for their future, as well as that of their family. The person who can provide hope during this time is going to be thought of fondly. Sometimes it is not even about pulling off a huge movement. At times, it is as simple as pointing out when something has gone right. Say the company has made a big sale. Talk about how much of a win that was.

Now while this is not about romantic attraction, I do want to visit the concept. What makes you attracted to a person? Of course, there is physical appearance, but what about their personality traits? Maybe they always have an aura of calm around them. Maybe they simply always help people out when they need it. You notice they are always there to help you up off of the floor when you finish a job that requires kneeling down. Maybe when you lose an item, they help you look for it. They always show regard for you when you walk into the room. They make you feel better when you have a bad day. These little gestures add up to an attractive person.

If you want something, you must attract it towards you. This concept goes for connecting to other people. This does not mean you insert yourself into their lives, but you need to create a presence in the world you want to be in.

Also, do not be afraid to seek help in creating a better self. Think about someone whose personality is attractive to you. Maybe they are a great public speaker. Ask them for tips on how to make your speeches better. Watch others to draw inspiration. You do not have to worry. This is not the same as copying. There are even people who make a career out of helping people become the best version of themselves. These people are known as life coaches, and it is worth looking into to spend some time with one. Also, look at all of the online sources you think will help you.

Be where you are right now. Whatever you are working on, give your all to that. If you are talking to someone and you are distracted with thoughts of your exam next week, it is going to show, and it will be unattractive to the person you are speaking to. You will have time to worry about that issue later. Focus on what is happening now. On the other hand, when you are studying for your exam, it is not the time to be thinking about the conversations you had earlier. When you are off somewhere else, you miss out on what is going on in the present. This might seem simple, but it is so easy for people's minds to wander off. That is the most attractive thing a person can be-present and alert. It gives off both an image of intelligence and caring. Employees will feel more confident, putting big projects into your hands. Friends will be more likely to choose you to talk to when they need advice. All of these things will add up to you having a more fruitful social life and career. Do not just watch your life happen to you. Decide what happens to it. Take an active role in your day. That is how you are going to get the most out of it.

CHAPTER 15

CREATE YOUR STORY BRAND

It would be great if we lived in a world without bias, but unfortunately, we do not. We will be more likely to believe information based on the source it comes from, and some of this is justified. For example, people find others who have a firm handshake to be more trustworthy, and often, it's true.

"How to become popular." You probably haven't thought about that since high school. However, this skill goes well beyond those four years. It is important to be well-liked. While it should not affect your every action, it would be erroneous to think it does not matter what other people think of you. In the workplace, those who make a good impression with their coworkers and potential bosses are more likely to be the successful candidate who gets the job and thrive in the work environment.

If you want to become more popular, the key is to be friendly and open. It is much less about being "cool" and more about being authentic. Being personable is a great start.

As you get to know people, share little bits of information about yourself. Of course, you would not tell them all of your secrets at once, but let pieces of your life and history slip into your conversation. This puts people at ease and feels like sharing things with you. It can be intimidating when you do not know anything about a person. At best, it can seem like you do not want to connect with other people, and at worst, people will think you have something to hide.

While you do not have to agree with others about everything, you need to be accepting of another's opinion. People dislike feeling judged and shot down about everything. There is a difference between stating your opinion and being overly opinionated and dogmatic.

When you see someone struggling with something, help them out. For example, someone is trying to move a heavy piece of furniture. Get on the other side of it. If you see someone drop something and it is near you, pick it up for them. These might seem like little gestures, but they mean a lot more to people than you might realize. One of the best compliments for a friend is that s/he is always willing to lend a hand. In the workplace, being considerate and helpful translates to being a good team player. This quality is so sought after that it generally appears as a part of the 360 review process.

Communication is not always verbal. When you do little favors for a person, you are sending them a message that says, "I see and care about you." Notice other's emotions and their state of well-being. If a friend comes in obviously feeling excited, ask them what has such a spring in their step so you can share in their elation. When it is obvious your friend could use a nice cheering up, do it. If you see that your co-worker is not feeling well, bring him/her a cup of tea.

To have connections, you have to build them. It takes two people to keep a running relationship of any sort. During the holidays, send them a message and ask them how they are doing. Suggest going out for lunch. If they are talking about a project, they need to do, offer your assistance. People remember that. If you talk about cooking a certain dish and your friend tells you they would love to learn that, offer to have them over and prepare it together. Invest your time and attention in others because it is a great way to broaden your horizons and live a more robust life.

Popular people speak their minds. Others do not have to wonder what they are thinking, and they tend to do what they say they are going to do. You can trust them to follow through.

Have you ever met someone and once you start talking, they talk about a certain hobby which makes you think about another friend? Make introductions to broaden your circle of friends.

No one gets along all the time, and part of good communication is the ability to disagree gracefully. In fact, if you have a problem with the way someone is treating you, you should be able to broach the subject and have a hard conversation without damaging the relationship. Maintain a respectful tone while getting your point across. A good communicator and a good friend knows how to set and keep boundaries. You do not have to say yes to everything.

Keep your conversation and attitude positive and make sure that words you speak about others remain upbeat. It does not take long for a group of friends or colleagues to identify the backstabber.

Be willing to get out of your comfort zone and try something new. Don't be afraid to do poorly at something you are unused to doing and laugh at yourself.

A popular person is generally mellow and even-tempered. All these qualities make a person more pleasant to be around, and more people will want to be around them. People want to be around others who know how to enjoy the spice of life.

If you want your business to take off, you need customers. This means you need to reach them.

This means you need to figure out who you are trying to appeal to. Let's say you are trying to start an IT business that helps people who are not as technically savvy. This means you need to have an approachable and friendly demeanor. While it might be nice to post an interesting tidbit of IT news sometimes, remember what your ultimate goal should be. Your goal is to reach out to people who do not know IT. Tell them what you can do for them. Talk to people in the demographic you are trying to reach. Ask them what their complaints are about IT support and what issues they are having with their devices. When you do get customers, cater to them. Check-in with them regularly and ask them how things are going for them, and if they need anything. People appreciate it when someone they are consistently paying keeps up consistent communication with them. This is how you get recommendations. When people they know talk about having technology issues, their minds will immediately jump to you, and they will encourage their friend to reach out to you. If this keeps up, you could have a stronghold in a particular town before you know it.

While you understandably want a potential client's business, you need to remember to talk to them like a person and not just a wad of cash. People can tell when you have this mentality because your dealings with them will begin to lack depth. While your client is not going to be your best friend, there is a long way between this and coming across as cold. Do not make it so that the only words that ever come out of your mouth are about business. This will make you seem robotic. Ask them how they are doing. If they told you some detail about their life, like getting a job offer, ask them how that is going. Then you let them know that you really see them as a person and pay special attention to their needs.

When you speak in a business situation, you need to be bold. While an employee needs to be respectful to their boss and put forward their best work, you cannot let yourself be railroaded by them. If you are not careful, you will be putting in more work than you are rewarded for. You will find that all of your time is taken up, and you cannot spend time with those you care about because your employer knows they can call you at any time, and you will drop everything. There must be boundaries. I understand that this is difficult because you are walking a thin line. You do not want to be insubordinate. You do not want anyone to be able to say that you are talking badly to your boss.

What, you might ask, is a brand story?

Essentially, it is a hook. When you hear that word, you probably think about what catches the audience's attention in a show, or a part in a song that makes it stand out. If you are conjuring up these images, you are on the right track. It is what gets people interested in your business. Imagine you are opening up a shoe store. You would need to ask yourself, why should customers choose my shoe store over all of the other ones that already exist? We cannot deny the emotional aspect that comes into play when we choose how to shop. Some people buy things from a collection simply for sentimental value. For example, it comes from something they loved as a child. There might be something about the business that gets them. There is something they stand for that speaks to them.

This is when you need to employ your brand story. Perhaps your store appeals to business, and you work toward helping people stand strong and confident as they tackle their business day.

It is important to have your brand story figured out before you launch your business. What type of emotion are you going to capture from your potential clients? Before we really begin our discussion, I want to assure you that this is not a bad thing. Any successful business person knows how to grab their audience through means of causing them to become emotionally invested. Think about what makes you become interested in a TV show and want to watch more. It might make you laugh, or frightened in a way that gives you a safe space to have a thrill, or it might be emotionally captivating because it addresses a problem many people face at some point during their life. You would never watch a movie all the way through if there was nothing to draw you in.

First, look back to your own story, meaning your personal life, and what has led you to this point. Do not sell yourself short. Many times we write ourselves off, thinking we do not have a good story to tell because we do not feel like anything interesting has happened in our lives or that we have had to overcome any problems. That is where our thinking becomes off. Your story does not have to be the most dramatic or crisis-filled to be interesting. Trace back to what got you started with this business.

Maybe it is something that has been passed down in your family. This itself will be appealing to people because that concept is endearing. People love to hear about loving families creating things together. You would be surprised at just how much personal opinions about the business owner can influence business deals.

Think about what you want your business to offer and how it is singularly effective in doing so. Maybe you have a clothing business that tailors each piece to be customized for every person. This will catch the attention of people who have a desire to be unique. They know they will never see another person wearing something like what they are wearing.

When you create a store brand, figure out what the people you are gearing towards will want. Moving on with the idea of a clothing business, some people will want to be unique, but there will also be people who want to wear things that are in as a means of helping their social standing. This could be your brand story, that the "popular people" wear your brand. This means your clothes will make your clients feel like they will be able to walk into the room and own the place.

Now, with that said, the store brand can work against you. Just as people can support you because of what you stand for, they can also withdraw said support for the same thing. Yes, business should stick to business, but that is, unfortunately, not the way the world works. This is why you need to think before you become a hard and boisterous advocate for something, especially when it is an extremely polarizing issue. This can cause you to alienate potential customers who do not feel like you would accept their business if you felt differently about it than they do. Even supporters can be turned off if the advocacy becomes too militant. Remember what you are trying to do. You want to create a successful business, not back a movement.

Finally, make your story brand authentic. Do not try to replicate what someone else has done, even if you idolize them. It worked for them because that is who they really are. No matter who you are, there is something unique and appealing about you. There is a struggle you have overcome that others would find admirable. There is a dynamic that would sell. You just really have to look.

CHAPTER 16

COMMUNICATION IN PUBLIC SPEAKING

Everyone gets a little nervous when they are speaking in public. You do not want to make a mistake. Don't worry. This will be easier than you think.

You will do yourself no good being worried about saying the wrong thing. This will happen from time to time. It has happened to the best of public speakers, and they came back from it. I can promise you that you will too. If it happens to you, the most important thing to do is to not make a big deal out of it. Do not run off stage or start making self-effacing remarks. You need to compose yourself and continue where you left off.

Be aware of your audience and its demographic. Keep that in mind as you craft your speech because you will want them to relate to you. Any humor you use should be tailored to the audience. Will you be outside or inside? In the sun or shade? Wear clothes that are comfortable and well-fitted, but not binding. You need to be able to move and not become too sweaty. Will you need a fan? This is not a time to wear "cruel shoes" Wear comfortable shoes that fit well.

You need to practice a lot. You may have cue cards, but you should largely know most of what you want to say. Be aware that things will happen during your speech. Not everyone may be quiet, and people may come and go. You need to be able to keep going without becoming flustered.

Practice in an area about the size of the stage you will speak on ultimately. Be able to use the space and create emphasis with your body movements and the method with which you walk around. Use a mirror so that you will be aware of your facial expressions. Make sure your eyes are soft and not bugged out, opened overly wide. Make sure your movements are natural. Practice in front of people, and while you want to maintain control of your speech, be open to suggestions.

Maintain eye contact with your audience. Make sure you distribute your attention across the crowd. Already, this will establish a connection with you and them.
Start with a thought-provoking question. This will get them in the right mindset to hear what you have to say. Learn the value of the pregnant pause. When you have made some big assertions, it will give the audience time to absorb what you have said before you pivot to something else.

Decide whether you will take questions, and if so, is it during your speech or if you will have a Q&A after your speech. Either way, maintain control so you will be able to begin and end on time.

You do not have to rush through your material. If you find yourself rushing through your speech to fit everything in, then you should consider trimming it down to have an easier gait. You may be asking too much of your audience as well. Perhaps you can be one step below mental athletics to listen to your speech.
Do not be afraid to give personal examples, even if they conjure emotion. This will create a sense of empathy between yourself and your audience that is tangible. You will see it on their faces when you have gotten to them. You will see a knowing look on their faces, and they will nod in agreement and/or approval.

Test your microphone and any visual equipment ahead of time. Nothing is more distracting and embarrassing than a big stop-gap before a speech.
Meditate or do some stretching before your speech. It will help

to clear your mind and make you feel more prepared for your speech.

Now that you have spent so much time and energy learning about your audience and your material. As well as all the practicing, you will go in with confidence. You are prepared, and you have thought of anything that could derail you. Trust in yourself, and have fun with it! You are going to do great in your public speaking experience.

CHAPTER 17

COMMUNICATION IN "ONE TO ONE" BUSINESS SALES

One on one communication happens in every aspect of life, whether you are talking to a family member, among colleagues, an authority figure, or among friends.
When you have a conversation with someone when you engage about something, and you both have aspects of consciousness to add to it, it is a joyful experience. The exchange of information and even the differences of opinion can be exciting.

Maintain eye contact with the person while they are speaking to you. This will assure them that you are still listening to them. Avoid distractions such as technology devices. When you are in a conversation with someone, be in that moment. Too often, our minds wander off to other places, which causes us not to be in the present. Just as you do when you meditate, turn off outside distractions. Stop your mind from veering off to other situations, or grocery lists, or what you need to do next week. Be present and give your attention fully to the person in front of you. Consider how unpleasant it is to speak with someone whose attention is wandering, and they are looking at their phones. Give your attention to the other person and expect the same respect.

Find occasional places to say the person's name. Everyone likes the sound of their name on another person's lips. It gives us the sense that the person cares about us when they do this. It also gives us the urge to use their name. It feels very intimate and conjures up a closeness between the two involved. It builds trust because it makes them feel acknowledged, and it feels personal.

There is a point at which you are doing it too much, however, so you do not want to come off creepy. However, sprinkling it into the conversation will keep them engaged and make them feel significant to you.

Ask them personal questions, thereby inviting them to talk openly about themselves. When I say this, I do not mean deeply personal ones. It can be as simple as asking them what kind of music they like. When they tell you, take some interest in it. Ask them if there is a particular song or artist that they like the most. This can be a springboard into a deep conversation where you learn about each other's favorite bands, ones you have seen in concert, and ones you want to see. When you share the reasons you like certain genres of music, bands, or songs, it will teach you about the other's personality.

When you are in a conversation with a new friend, have you ever learned something that you have in common, and one or the other laughs out, "I do that too!" It creates an instant closeness, and you both smile. While we all enjoy the challenge and learning experience of people who are different than we are, there is a special connection between two people who have some of the same likes and dislikes.

When you learn something about someone that is a matter of pride for them, congratulate them, compliment them, it will make them feel special. When you are open to someone in that way, they will find it easier to do the same with you.

Be an active listener. Let the other person talk and do not wait to talk. Pay attention to them. People are aware when your mind is speeding ahead, and you are not really absorbing what they say while you play over and over in your mind what you want to say next. Everyone likes to feel important, and when someone asks our opinion, it means that they regard us highly.

Business sales are tricky to do successfully.

First, you want to avoid trying too hard to sell your product. This might sound strange because this is what you are trying to do, but think about a time when you were at the store and you were pulled aside by a salesperson, or when a telemarketer called you. It is automatically off-putting for a person when it is blatantly obvious to them that you are trying to get something from them. It will cause them not to trust what you say. Nobody likes the hard sell tactic.

Start a regular conversation with them first. It does not have to be a long, drawn-out one. It should just be an ice breaker. Move on from there to questions that will help you learn about your potential client's problems that are relative to your solutions you are trying to sell. You need to become a confidant for your client. You want them to think of your face when they have a problem because they know you are interested in helping them.

Otherwise, you be thought of as that widget salesperson, and they only think of you when they need that particular widget. Consider an Avon salesperson who comes to your door, and you know about the "Skin So Soft" product as being an effective bug repellent, so you buy some. If s/he does not strike up a conversation with you, s/he may not know that you are concerned about acne and an uneven skin tone, for which she could suggest solutions. A month later, after trying the products, you are feeling great about your complexion. Since s/he has built a rapport with you, they call you and learn that you are going on vacation for which you need a good sunscreen and that you want something that will brighten your skin so you will look your best when you go. See how that works? When you have a relationship with a person, and they feel you are interested in what is happening with them and can offer a fix for them, you have moved up a level in the client's mind.

Even if a client comes to you with a problem that your solutions do not solve, do your best to help them. Your products may be part of an overall solution for them or at any rate. You have proved yourself to be concerned with the well-being of their business.

Communication is about more than the words your client says. You need to read his/her non-verbal communication and listen to the tone of their voice. Your best time to make a sales pitch is not when the person is in a hurry and irritable. There is a look in someone's eye when they are unable to absorb what you are saying, they may fidget, and you can sense in their energy that they cannot be sold right now, and you need to learn that look. They will appreciate your sensitivity, and that will strengthen the relationship.

Be aware of and in control of your own body language as well. Avoid inadvertently doing things that suggest dishonesty, such as touching or rubbing your face, throat, or eyes. Be actively present, not eyeing the door like you want to escape. Make sure your handshake is firm, but this is not a contest, do not over-squeeze and hurt them. Look them in the eye and keep it short unless the other party does not let go. Usually, people shake with their right hand. However, if the person offer's their left, go with it. Try not to fidget because that implies anxiety or boredom, even hyperactivity.

The small things mean a lot to people. You should not do it every time, but sometimes a tiny gift can remind them of you during the day and keep you top of mind. If there is some way you can help them, then do so.

Another type of sale is the cold-call. This is when you do not know the person you are selling to. It's quite difficult, and many people consider it a nuisance. However, if that is your job, you need to learn to do it successfully. Greet the person and identify yourself quickly. Humor can help to smooth things over and keep them on the phone. Get to the point quickly, however, and your effort should be how you can help them. You need to be assertive, but not obnoxious, so try to make the sale, but know whether the call is over.

Lastly, everyone needs to learn to deal with an unhappy customer. Maybe they are upset because they feel that something is different than how they feel it was agreed upon with you. Bring your A-game in terms of listening. You should not bad mouth your company, but let the client know you understand how they feel, and you can put yourself in their place. Apologize to the customer and make sure they feel heard, however, move quickly towards solution-mode. Let them know if you need to research the issue internally, but assure them you are working hard to solve the problem and that you will keep them in the loop every step of the way.

CHAPTER 18

COMMUNICATION IN MEETINGS

There are several different personalities we all have to take on, depending on what situation we are in at the time. In a meeting, such as for work, for your Parent Teacher Organization or your Homeowner's Association, or even a book club, there is a specific way you will want to be perceived. You want to be seen as intelligent, alert, and well-spoken.

When you are at a business meeting, you want to uphold a professional persona. However, you do not want to overdo it, or you will come across as uptight, which can make others around you feel uncomfortable and less willing to open up. Do not be afraid to display your own personality. Be yourself.

Don't overthink it. Be aware of the image you want to present in polite company. Avoid the slang and jokes you would use around your closest friends. When you come to a meeting, show up on time, having read any materials you were assigned. Have a smile on your face and a positive attitude. Greet everyone pleasantly, and if there is someone in attendance who you do not know, introduce yourself to them.

Be open to receiving information, and do not make negative comments. This is not to say that offering suggestions is off-limits, but make them in the spirit of helpfulness.
When you are in a meeting, and someone else is presenting, listen to the speaker. Give them the benefit of your attention, and do not talk to others, thereby distracting them, so they also do not hear. Take notes, but listen more than you write and certainly do

not doodle the whole time.

Remember, it takes a lot of courage to stand up and speak in front of others. You would want people to pay attention since you had taken the time to prepare something. If you have questions, raise your hand. If the speaker is willing to stop and take questions during his/her presentation, s/he will call on you. Even if the speaker does take questions, try not to interrupt too much, let the speaker get through their prepared speech. If the speaker does not want to take questions until the end, s/he will say there is a question and answer segment afterward. Respect that. Write down your questions so you will not forget them and be sure to wait for your turn.

If you are the speaker, be prepared. It is disrespectful to your audience to come unprepared. It is best if you practice, maybe even in front of another person, maybe a family member who you can trust to give you honest feedback.

If there is someone who does not speak much during the meeting, try to draw them out, they may not even realize that they have something to contribute. Always be respectful of others in the meeting, even when they say something you either find irrelevant or you disagree with the point they are making.

During your meeting, turn off your electronic devices. This is not a time to be reading and responding to emails, and a phone ringing is such a distraction.

Also, be aware of your body language. This is not a time to display any behaviors that mean bored, such as the exaggerated yawn, looking around too much, and being obvious about your wandering attention. This is not a time for a nap or putting your head down. Watch your facial expressions to make sure they remain positive and interested. Lean into the meeting, physically, and your mind will follow.

No one likes to be called out publicly, and at your meeting is not the time to call someone out by name stating something that they have done wrong. Now is the time to focus on finding solutions for problems, not to create strains on relationships. Remember, these are people you will need to work with, and maybe even a favor from in the future.

Watch your language during a meeting. Nothing makes you look worse than cursing.

What if someone asks you a question you do not know the answer to? Try not to become frustrated and start stammering. Instead, acknowledge that this is a relevant question and promise to send the attendees that information at a later date. This should happen at the soonest opportunity. If you ask someone something, they do not know the answer to, behave in an empathetic manner and do not berate them for not knowing the answer. Accept that they can send everyone the information later. Offer help if needed.

Try not to interrupt the agenda of the meeting too much. Remember, you have already specified duration for the meeting, so you want to be respectful of everyone's time. Meetings run long sometimes, but try not to get off course. Try not to start talking to someone about another topic that should be taken "offline" and talked about at another time.

It is all about respect for others in your meeting, including administrative or janitorial staff. Do not leave a mess since your meeting room may be booked directly after your own session.

CHAPTER 19

COMMUNICATION ON SOCIAL MEDIA

Social media has become such an important part of our lives in modern times. A business needs an online presence to succeed. Social media profiles are checked by potential employers and can be a make-or-break for applicants. Your social media presence is your personal branding tool. You have probably seen the recent litany of people being called into question about social media posts from their pasts.

Gone are the days that our pasts can be hidden. When you post something on the internet, it is always going to be there. This is why you need to really think it over before you leave something on social media. Ask yourself some questions:

- Would I want my relatives, boss, or other significant people in my life to see this?
- Is this something I can endorse with a clear conscience?
- Am I sharing too much personal information of my own or someone else?
- Is it true? Is it kind? Would you describe it as useful or harmful?

Many people are suffering the consequences of having posted something they thought was funny or shocking at the moment, but now it is a permanent part of their history. This is why it is advisable to keep more unflattering statements within your personal conversations with trusted friends.

Make sure you keep an upbeat persona when you leave social

media messages.

This might be challenging when you are addressing heavy subject matter, which for some platforms has to be done. To learn how to tread this water, think about how deeply you have to go into the subject when you are showcasing the headlines for it. Is the headline inflammatory or easily misunderstood?

Arguing over social media is ill-advised, as is calling someone out in a shaming tactic. That is not brave. It would be far braver to have a personal conversation with the person and hash it out one on one. You involve other people, and it is not their business. You hurt yourself most if you do this, however, because it portrays you in a bad light. Try to see things from the other person's point of view and ask yourself if you would like it if someone posted the same thing about you.

Decide what your social media brand will be. Some stick with cute posts about kittens and puppies and keep it positive. That's a good policy because it will not offend anyone. Everyone sometimes slips, however, because they feel passionate about something.

If you put something on social media, make sure that it comes from a place in you that is compassionate. Avoid posting anything if you have been drinking. If you are under the influence, put away your phone and computer. You cannot adhere to your social media brand if you are impaired. You may say something you could regret. Things on social media cannot be taken back. You may think something is funny or relevant at the time, but will it stand the test of time? Or will you damage relationships and other's perceptions of you?

It is okay to state your opinion and share your views, but be sensible. Also, keep vulgarity to a minimum. Everyone lets their guard down around friends and is less guarded about their language with them, and it is normal to do so. However, remember that your social media can and will be reviewed by potential employers.

Another aspect of empathy in social media is to refrain from posting another's secrets on social media. You should not complain about friends or family. Alternately, if you are having a conversation with someone, be present and not on social media at that moment. If you need to talk about problems you are having with another person, keep that offline. Call someone and have a private discussion about it. It does not go over well for people to see you speaking ill of someone online or revealing personal conversations. Sometimes when you try to make another person look bad in the eyes of others, this will wind up backfiring on you. They will read your comments and be wary of you. They will wonder if certain parts were exaggerated or even fabricated, as we have the potential to do whenever we are upset. They will also be hesitant to tell your personal things or get too close because they do not want their personal information aired out for everyone to read.

A general rule for social media posting is to keep things positive. You can even voice your opinions on issues. You do not have to be a completely neutral and inscrutable person. Just keep from ranting or attacking someone's character. If you want to show pride in political figures you admire, go ahead. Just keep it an upbeat tribute to them instead of a jab at someone you do not like as much because these types of posts rarely go over well. Always keep a sense of mindfulness when you post something. Make sure you have good motivations to do so, and that what you say online goes with how you want to be perceived in real life.

CHAPTER 20

COMMUNICATION ON SOCIAL VIDEO

These days, people can make entire careers out of streaming videos of themselves just talking to an audience. However, to be successful at it, you must really know how to go about it.

If you want to have consistent followers, they must feel like you appreciate having them around. For many people, they join these streams to feel a sense of belonging with other people. They see the speaker and those watching with them as a group of friends. Acknowledge that so you validate their feelings. Greet them at the beginning, and wish them a good day at the end.

Many video streams have live chats. Respond to some of those who contribute to it. You do not have to respond to every single comment. Not only would this be impossible, but it would derail your flow of thought. If a question keeps appearing from multiple people, this is one to address. Give shoutouts to some of the commenters. When you do these things, it will mean a lot to them. It will confirm their idea that they are part of a group.
Now let's talk about when you do not have a chat to interact with. Even though you are speaking by yourself, you are still trying to connect with an audience, so you need to keep them in mind.

When you are speaking this way, it is easy to lose sight of the fact that you are speaking to other people. This can make your voice, and body language come across as overly rehearsed and robotic. To combat this, think of the camera as a person you are talking to. Get accustomed to the idea that it is the recipient of your thoughts. This way, you will remain engaged.

The internet has proven to be a double-edged sword in communication. On one hand, it has made it easier for us to start a conversation with people, and it makes us able to get in touch with those we would never have been able to reach otherwise. However, it can be easy to forget that you are talking to actual people. If you are going to be a content creator on a website, you will need to build a platform for yourself. This means you need to zero in on a target audience and find a niche for yourself.

Say you want to create a comedy channel. In this case, empathy will be especially important. Comedy aims to evoke the emotional reaction of laughing out of someone. This means you need to know what will make people laugh, and this is particularly difficult because that is a moving target. What made people laugh a decade ago could be considered offensive now. You need to feel out the climate of your target audience if you want to be successful.

Contrary to the somewhat popular opinion, comedy is not about saying the most shocking and off-color thing you can think of. Actually, many times people laugh the most at jokes that relate to real life. This is why you need to get to know your target audience. What are most of them doing? What struggles are they facing? Many times, making light of the harsher situation we face can be a means of coping with it, because laughing at it can create a tone that is less harsh.

CHAPTER 21

COMMUNICATION ON WEB SITES

So you want to start a website. If you want to have followers, you will need to appeal to people. This means while you are designing your website and thinking about aesthetics, you need to place equal importance on how you communicate with your audience. Empathy can guide you to properly reaching potential clients. First, you need to make your website easy to navigate. Is this website for a business or an information-driven one? Be sure that you are clear about your mission and/or product and service offering.

I would avoid too many stock photographs because they lack the ability to let your personality shine through. Best in class websites tend to be current and have current personal messages as a matter of course.

Too many pop-ups can be frustrating for the visitor and cause them to back out of your site reflexively, fearing that they will get a computer virus. However, requesting information about visitors is fine, particularly if you give them the assurance that their information will not be given or sold to others and that they can opt-out easily if it becomes cumbersome.

People love the communication that seems personal and relevant. Too many pictures and things that gobble up their bandwidth is frustrating, whereas a short message that is concise and contains the person's name. Avoid sending mass communications to people.

Why are you contacting the person? Is it because they have made a particular purchase on your site, and you want to make them aware of a particular sale? The point is, let the person know how you are trying to benefit them.

Many companies have excellent examples of thoughtful ways to communicate with their customers, such as Guitar Center. They tend to send personal "signed" notes that contain coupons exclusively for previous customers. Also, Dollar General has created an app allowing customers to clip coupons that are redeemed at the point of sale, and you can even tally up your order as you go. Do you see how that would give the customer the perception that they are in control as well as getting a discount?

You might offer free live webinars where something specific can be discussed or where some training can be attained. Have the person sign up, and in that way, you will have some contact information from them. Try to make the session interactive because you may attain even more information from a select few attendees about what their needs are and how you may help them.

Importantly, avoid over-communicating, which can cause people to opt-out, thus losing them as potential clients or members.

Even in this digital world, some people prefer phone conversations. Even if they are very comfortable communicating through chat and other digital means, there comes the point where the client must talk to a live person. That process should not be a hassle. Nobody likes to be on hold for a long time, and a confusing interactive voicemail system creates a less than a delightful experience. If the person needs to leave a voicemail, make sure the call is returned within a business day.

Receiving an email summarizing each type of interaction is helpful. That way, the person does not have to record and keep up with confirmation numbers, and there is agreement about whatever transaction or agreement occurred during the call.

Make sure clients do not have to hunt for buttons they need to shop, purchase, or edit their shopping cart. Test the process for yourself because if it is cumbersome and frustrating for you, then your customer will have a similar experience.

Everyone loves feeling like they have gotten a deal, so remember holidays and throw in a little discount or special gift. This type of practice can translate into wonderful word-of-mouth advertising for you. People like to feel special.

Make a place for customer reviews and/or suggestion box. In particular, never let negative reviews hang out in cyberspace unanswered. Go out of your way to connect with that customer and make them feel heard and properly reimbursed. Ask for a chance to earn their business again. When that happens, make sure this customer gets a peak experience. In addition, use negative remarks to make things better for all of your customers.

CHAPTER 22

COMMUNICATION ON INSTANT MESSAGING

Instant messaging is a much more intimate communication method than you would think. However, in many ways, it is trickier than speaking face to face.

When it comes to instant messaging, shorter is better most of the time. When you leave a long, wordy message, it will be more difficult for the person to take in. They might miss out on important pieces of information because people tend to gloss over large pieces of text instead of reading the whole thing.

With this in mind, stick to the most important facts. Leave out unnecessary detail.

It is best to say things literally when you are talking through messaging. This is because you cannot convey the tone of voice and facial expression through text. Therefore, sarcastic comments or nuanced jokes might not come through to the receiver. This can lead to a miscommunication or someone thinking you were saying something seriously when you were not.

Instant messaging is inevitably part of how we communicate today. It is in real-time, but there are breaks in it because if you get a call in the middle of instant messaging one person and speak to the one on the phone, your instant message conversation is put on hold. Everyone does it, but you should tell the other person that you will be out of pocket for a bit. Use the same manners you would if it were a face to face talk.

Start the conversation with a brief greeting and ask if this is a good time to talk. Keep it lighthearted. Instant messaging is a bad place to argue. Mainly because even face to face, people tend to communicate poorly when they are upset. When perturbed, one is generally more prone to wait to talk rather than genuinely listen to what the other is saying. It is very easy to read the first few words, assume you know the point the other person is making and launch right into your own tirade.

Also, remember that when you are writing an instant message, there is a record of everything you say. If you type harsh words or even insults, the person will very likely read and reread them. There is a difference between thinking about an argument and playing it over again in your mind and seeing it in black and white. Being able to read over it can keep it going longer than it should, and because you do not see the person, you each may become freer with your words than you should. Another reason why quarreling is a bad idea over instant message is the fact that it can be shown to others. Do not engage in disagreements by instant message.

Another thing to avoid when instant messaging is to deliver unfortunate news. This is not a medium that you should use to break up with someone or tell them about a loss. You may not know where the person is when you message with them or what they are doing or are about to do. If they are driving, and though they should not look at messages at the time, if they do, they could have an accident. If they are at work, they could make a mistake that could be costly for them. The empathetic response at that time is to wait until you can at least speak to them directly over the phone or, preferably, face to face.

Except in specific circumstances, it is best not to instant message someone you do not know. This excludes customer service people, of course. People also use dating apps, and meeting people tends to start with instant messaging. However, use caution in those conversations. Do not give them personal or financial information. If it appears you can never personally meet them, do not let them take up too much of your time and attention. Concentrate more on someone you can have a real relationship with.

If you are talking to a customer service representative, remember that you are speaking to a real person with feelings and emotions. Most people will go out of their way to help you if you are compassionate with them.

When you are instant messaging with someone, try not to use too many abbreviations because not everyone knows all of them. Some abbreviations are fine, but try your best to type out words and use complete sentences. Make your tone nice and kind. You do not have to be rigid, but try to use good grammar.

Also, be patient, giving the other person ample time to respond to you before you launch into another question. Instant message conversations can become confusing and tedious if you do that. Make sure the other person understands your first point before you go on to the next one.

Unless you are on a group chat, avoid having two conversations at once. First, it is rude, and second, you can confuse conversations giving the wrong information to someone. This behavior can hurt someone's feelings should they realize you are having another conversation simultaneously.

Finish your chat by saying something nice, wish the other person a good day, and tell them you enjoyed speaking with them. It is also a good time to plan your next visit.

CHAPTER 23

HOW TO ORGANIZE A WINNING BUSINESS SPEECH

You might think a short speech is easier to perform than a long one, but it comes with its own sets of challenges. For one, you have to pack more information into a shorter time constraint and make it flow naturally. You do not want to jump from topic to topic, making your speech erratic. You also have a shorter time to make an impact.
On the bright side, you do not have to worry about holding your audience's attention for a long time.

When you are putting a short speech together, you need to understand that you are dealing with a limited amount of time. Have you ever been writing a paper for a class and wondered how you were going to create enough content for the word count only to get to the end and realize you do not have enough room to cover every part of the subject? This means you need to zero in on one topic and make everything you say relate to it. If you try to tackle more issues than your allotted time can successfully address, you will have said a lot in a short time without actually covering any ground.

Remember that a speech is not just to introduce a problem. You need to offer a solution to it. Let's say you are calling a meeting to talk about the fact that there has been less productivity than usual in the workplace. You cannot just say, "our business is declining, and this needs to stop." Figure out how this can happen. Cover a few possible motivators. You do not need to cover every single one. In fact, if you do this, it will be overwhelming for your listeners. Write down three solutions and give them equal coverage. End on a positive note, such as "I look forward to seeing our company being restored to its usual self." This will help people feel motivated.

Even if you are calling a meeting about a problem, you do not have to make the tone somber. Do not make threats of anyone losing their job or being on notice. People who anxious will not be motivated. Create an optimistic picture. Try presenting it with this message- we haven't been performing at our usual level, but now is our chance to get ourselves back on track. Again, the use of the word "we" is important. It will make your employees feel more connected with you, and they will appreciate you taking part in the ownership. If the people have been underperforming across the board, this is a sign that there has been a decline in leadership. When you own up to this, your employees will actually gain respect for you. You might think you are showing signs of weakness to them, but from their point of view, it will be you acknowledging that you are human, and instead of standing over them and placing all of the blame on them you are trying to work with them, both sides improving their behaviors.

While you do want to maintain a professional tone, do not be afraid to let a well-placed joke slip out. By well-placed, I mean relevant to the subject of your speech. This can put the recipients of your speech at ease. However, the caveat is that it must tie into a point. For example, you could have a one-liner at the beginning of your speech that serves as a springboard for the topic of your speech, and then hold off on them.

Now, I want to talk about preparation. The quality of a speech is influenced by what happens to it beforehand. You would think a short speech would mean you need to think about it less, right? Wrong. The time constraint means there is more pressure on you to get your point across within a short amount of time. There is an age-old method, sometimes known as the 80/20 method. This means you write down a bunch of content and leave 80 percent of it out, leaving only 20 percent of quality material that you keep. This will ensure that your speech will be informative but short and sweet. In long speeches, you can afford to have a little fluff or filler material, but the same rule does not apply to short speeches. Any filler words you have taken up time that could be filled with key information.

When you make a speech, you need to pull your audience into it. Otherwise, it will look like you are just talking at them. Recognize individuals for their contributions. Emphasize the idea that you want this to be a group effort. Make yourself one of them. This will let your employees know that you do not just see them as replaceable commodities. People are not as motivated to work when they do not think they are seen other than when they do something wrong. As with any speech, remember what you are trying to convey. Keep your tone according to and your information relevant.

We've talked about what makes short speeches difficult. Now it is time to learn how to navigate through a lengthy one.

In good news, you have the freedom to address more ideas in greater depth. However, the challenge is keeping them interesting. You need to keep from being repetitive.
First, you need to plan what you are going to talk about. This will help prevent you from rambling or getting off-topic, which are the two biggest risks when giving a long speech.
Do not feel ashamed about bringing notecards with your talking points jotted down onto it. This does not mean you do not know your stuff. It just means you have come prepared. If you need to look at them for reference, they are available. They will also help you stay on track because you will have a visual of the points you still need to get across. You will have a more natural and organized flow. You might look down at your notecards and realize you are starting to talk on a little too long about a particular point, and it is time to move on to the next one because you have seen

how much you still have left to talk about. Conversely, you might see that you almost missed an important topic.

If you go back to a point, make sure you expand upon it. If you are trying to convince your audience that a certain drink has health benefits and you go back to the fact that it possibly helps insomnia, make sure you give new information about that. Perhaps tell them what it will mean for their energy levels, productivity, and physical and mental health if they get proper sleep. When you handle it this way, you will succeed in further driving home your point.

Long speeches are infamous for being breeding grounds for unnecessary information. It is easy to go off on a tangent about something that is not relevant for the point you are trying to make. It is one thing to make a quick joke and then get back on track. It is one thing to tell a long story about an outing with you and your friend that does not contribute to the message of the speech. As a rule of thumb, if you are going to tell a story, make it make sense for your speech. Maybe talk about how you and your friend drank this juice and found that you were able to run a mile more than you usually do, or how by the end of the day, you did not feel tired.

Engage with your audience. Otherwise, it will be hard to hold their attention just by talking to them for an hour. Even if they are just rhetorical questions, ask them. This makes them part of the discussion instead of just a bystander. Perhaps you ask them to write down a set of goals they want to accomplish this month.

When you are giving a speech, do not be afraid of the pregnant pause. For one, this can give you time to collect your thoughts. When you have been speaking for a long time, it is easy to get your words jumbled up. It can also be used to emphasize a point, and when used right, it can increase the power of your statement.

You would be surprised as to how much work talking for a long time is. It will wreak havoc on your voice and throat if you do not take care of it. If you watch any representative deliver a lengthy speech, you will notice they have a cup of water near them. Make sure you have one and make use of it any time you need it. You do not want to lose your voice or have a sore throat the next day because of this. If you need just to rest your voice for a moment, allow yourself to do so.

Do some research before you take on this task. Watch public figures who are known for their great speeches. You will see that they do not just stand on a podium and talk for an hour. That would be boring. Those speakers talk with their hands and face. When you are describing an event, use your hands to help paint the picture. Maybe you are talking about something that happened at the beach. To take the audience there, you could comment on the water and make a motion with your hands that mimic the tide.

You can use the energy of the audience as inspiration and go to your next talking point. Sometimes you will need an idea. You cannot realistically expect yourself to completely rehearse a speech that goes on for an hour or even longer. If you notice someone has a question, do not be afraid to ask them. They might give you an angle to come at the subject you would not have thought of before. Remember that you would not have a speech if you did not have an audience. If you keep yourself in contact with them, you will have a better speech than you could have hoped for.

CONCLUSION

You have everything you need to hone your empathy and use it to your advantage. You don't even need to acquire something you do not already have; you know how to talk to others in a way that shows compassion. You know how to feel for others. You can tell based on facial and nonverbal cues how a person is reacting to something you said. Now all you have to do is practice all of these skills until they become second nature to you.

When we learn how to connect with others, we are doing right by ourselves and everyone around us. In time, as you put these methods into practice, you will enjoy much more healthy and peaceful relationships. You will also be able to appeal to your employers and other people it would benefit you to impress.

You will notice every aspect of your life is changing, as you deepen your bonds with others. People are willing to go greater lengths for those who they like. If you need someone to put in a good word for you as you are applying for a job or other organization, it will be much easier to find someone to do this. You will find that you have those people you can call when you are having a bad day.

Empathy isn't just a feeling. It is the words you say and the things you do. It comes down to asking yourself, "would I like it if someone said or did this to me?" Then you make your decision based on your answer.